CONT

A word about terminology. The foundational documents of Methodism (The Deed of Union, Standing Orders) refer to 'The Lord's Supper', whereas the term used in the Methodist Worship Book is 'Holy Communion'. In ecumenical circles, the word 'Eucharist' is generally employed. In this report, we will generally speak of 'Holy Communion' or simply 'Communion' unless the context suggests another term, as this is the predominant usage in British Methodism today (see paragraphs 30-31).

'HIS PRESENCE MAKES THE FEAST'

Holy Communion in the Methodist Church

Jesus, we thus obey
Thy last and kindest word;
Here, in thine own appointed way,
We come to meet thee, Lord.

Our hearts we open wide
To make the Saviour room;
And lo! The Lamb, the crucified,
The sinner's friend, is come!

His presence makes the feast;
And now our spirits feel
The glory not to be expressed,
The joy unspeakable.

With pure celestial bliss
He doth our spirits cheer;
His house of banqueting is this,
And he hath brought us here.

He bids us drink and eat
Imperishable food;
He gives his flesh to be our meat,
And bids us drink his blood.

Whate'er the almighty can
To pardoned sinners give,
The fullness of our God made man
We here with Christ receive.

Charles Wesley (1707-1788)
Hymns & Psalms 614

A SUMMARY AND CONCLUSIONS

As an aid to study, suggested questions for discussion are included throughout the report in this colour and style of text.

1
Methodism inherited from John and Charles Wesley a devout appreciation of Holy Communion as a divinely appointed means of grace. The undefined but real presence of Christ was proclaimed in their sermons and hymns. The Wesleys taught an understanding of the eucharistic sacrifice as one in which the offering of the obedient hearts and lives of the communicants was united by grace to the perfect, complete, ever-present and all-atoning sacrifice of Christ. John Wesley adapted the liturgy of the Book of Common Prayer (at first for use in the American missions) and this was later widely used in the Wesleyan Methodist tradition. In other branches of Methodism, the form of worship was closer to that of other Free Churches.

2
The early Methodists were expected to practise constant and frequent Communion, either at the parish church (although in the first century of Methodism, 1740 to 1840, it was not the custom to celebrate Communion every week in most parish churches) or in their own chapels, receiving Communion either from Church of England clergy or, later, from their own itinerant preachers (ministers). However, in each of the branches of Methodism before the 1932 union, the number of Sunday congregations far exceeded the number of such ministers. This was usually the main reason why the Lord's Supper continued to be celebrated no more than monthly in the town chapels and usually only quarterly in the villages.

3
Today Methodists vary hugely in their attachment to Holy Communion. For some it is at the very heart of their discipleship, for some it is one treasured means of grace among others and for a small minority of Methodists Communion is not perceived as either desirable or necessary.

4
There is a wide diversity of practice in Methodist churches across the Connexion. Such differences reflect, to some extent, the different historical traditions that have come together to form the present day Methodist Church. Having somewhat

diverse roots, it is not surprising that British Methodism as a whole has not developed a unified set of practices in respect of the celebration of the Lord's Supper. Though clearly peripheral in some of the historical strands of Methodism, this service has more recently come, on a practical level, to play a more central role in the life of the whole Church.

5
The 1999 *Methodist Worship Book*, officially authorised and widely (though not universally) used throughout the Methodist Church, reflects both biblical insights and historic traditions of the universal Church in the content and liturgical shape of the several services set out for Holy Communion for different seasons and occasions.

6
As to a Methodist theology of the Holy Communion, in spite of distinguished work by individual scholars, it could be said that Methodist doctrine has received little *official* formulation and exists more as an undefined (or under-defined) tradition. The theology is implicit in the liturgies, hymns and the practical arrangements for Holy Communion. It should also be noted that there are tensions between what has been said by the various members of the world-wide Methodist family at different times and in different places. For example, there were differences between the responses of the British Methodist Church and the United Methodist Church to the World Council of Churches' Lima Report *Baptism, Eucharist and Ministry* (1982) (*Churches Respond to Baptism, Eucharist and Ministry*, World Council of Churches 1986).

7
Two alternative conclusions can be drawn from this. Either Methodism has signally failed by default to respond to the desire of other Churches for fuller definition (or doctrinal development) and perhaps doesn't know what it believes; or it has deliberately maintained a proper reserve and agnosticism on some issues – at least in some circumstances. It can, however, be firmly said that Methodists have always sought to base their belief and practice in respect of the Lord's Supper on thoroughly biblical foundations. Even so, this has been with a variety of emphases and interpretations and has only in recent years taken account of the full spectrum of eucharistic texts and liturgical principles.

8
Strictly speaking, 'Holy Communion' is, in Methodist understanding, a service that includes *both* Word and Sacrament (even though the *Methodist Worship Book* denotes

one section of it as 'the Lord's Supper', and it is on the latter that this report concentrates). This report identifies (paragraphs 147-194) nine essential components or themes of the Methodist Church's theology of Holy Communion. In each case, the authors of this report have attempted to find a word or phrase that expresses the theme in everyday language, as well as indicating the more technical terms that may lie behind them:

- thanksgiving (Eucharist)
- life in unity (*koinonia*)
- remembering (*anamnesis*)
- sacrifice
- presence
- the work of the Spirit (*epiclesis*)
- anticipation (eschatology)
- mission and justice
- personal devotion.

9
As Methodists, we wish to maintain those insights that have developed within our own tradition and to share these with others. At the same time, we wish to remain faithful to the apostolic tradition shared by all Christians. We believe that Christian theology continually develops as new insights are received, both within and beyond Methodism. The theology of Holy Communion does not develop in isolation from the rest of theology. Understanding of Holy Communion has received a new emphasis through the rediscovery of sacramental theology (the idea that God communicates through physical realities). It has been argued that Christ is the original sacrament and by derivation, Christ's body the Church is the sacrament of God's presence in the world. Some have talked of the way in which Holy Communion 'makes' the Church. The 1999 Conference statement on the nature of the Church, *Called To Love and Praise (CLP)* holds that 'the Eucharist, in particular, both focuses and expresses the ongoing and the future life of the Church' (*CLP* 2.4.8.). Part of the uniqueness of Holy Communion lies in its use of a particularly wide range of the senses – touch and taste as well as sight and hearing.

10
For Methodists, there are some issues surrounding the Lord's Supper that arise from the diversity within our own tradition. Other matters to do with Holy Communion arrive on the Methodist agenda, as both formal and informal ecumenism present us

with the eucharistic faith and practice of other Christian Churches. This is particularly important as we consider those with whom we would one day desire either much closer relations or organic union.

11
Internally, along with most other Christian traditions, Methodists would benefit from a programme of thorough and high quality teaching concerning the meaning and value of Holy Communion and its place in our spiritual lives. Such teaching would not be seeking to impose uniformity; rather it should take account of the diversity of belief and practice within our Church, acknowledging that some issues have been (and in some cases remain) controversial. It is not just about the nourishment of the individual pilgrim but also about seeing Holy Communion as a means of creating and expressing Christian fellowship.

12
Methodists also need to grasp afresh that Holy Communion can be a starting point in an effective pursuit of mission and justice, matters that we have traditionally pursued with great vigour.

B INTRODUCTION

13
'The Methodist Church recognises two sacraments, namely Baptism and the Lord's Supper, as of divine appointment and of perpetual obligation of which it is the privilege and duty of members of the Methodist Church to avail themselves.' *(Deed of Union, Clause 4)* It may seem surprising then that never, in over seventy years since Methodist union, has the Church attempted to set down in detail what it believes and practises when its people gather to share bread and wine in 'Holy Communion.' Of course, the hymns and liturgies we use imply much, as do the ways in which the worship resources authorised by the Conference have been compiled. This report attempts to address the lack of a more explicit description of the Methodist position, but does not pretend to be a 'definitive', far less 'final' word on the subject.

14
The report proceeds from the observation that for Methodists, theology often arises from reflection on practice rather than beginning with 'abstract' theories. John Wesley's *method* of 'practical theology' is still central to Methodism, which is at heart a method of responding to God's gracious offer of salvation and holiness. In order to know what Methodists believe it is necessary to look at what they do, for they are truest to themselves when they express, transmit and modify their beliefs in the context of the worshipping, learning, serving and witnessing life of the faith community – in the Church and in the wider world.

15
In consequence of this, in order to find out what Methodists believe and do it is necessary to go behind official statements and policies. This necessity arises, we believe, not because Methodism is a peculiarly disorderly tradition (far from it) but because its original motivation of having 'nothing to do but save souls' persists in the form of a strong desire that worship shall be *effective*. *Called to Love and Praise* notes the importance of experience in the Methodist tradition *in the area of worship*. The desire that worshippers shall *experience* a sense of 'wonder, love and praise' explains the existence of both connexionally authorised forms and significant local variations in Methodist worship. It also makes it necessary to investigate what worshippers actually experience. Therefore, this report offers a snapshot of Methodist practice at the start of the twenty-first century (with an eye to the wider ecumenical and historical contexts). It then offers some resources that inform and are informed by the underlying theology.

16

It is not the purpose of this report to set out the limits of what is acceptable. It describes 'how things are' rather than prescribing how things 'ought' or 'ought not' to be. It is offered to the Methodist people and to our ecumenical partners as an aid to understanding who we are and what we believe and do in relation to Holy Communion.

17

The report was prepared for the Faith and Order Committee by a small working party that consulted widely, in particular through the distribution of a questionnaire about belief and practice, and through an invitation to individuals, churches and circuits, to submit their views and experiences in writing. In the end over 400 questionnaires were returned, and over 80 other written responses received. These have greatly informed what follows and immense gratitude is due to all who contributed in these ways. The working party also drew upon the previous statements and publications of the Conference, international and ecumenical documents and the writings of Methodist scholars.

18

The members of the working party were: David Carter, Robert Dolman, Norman Graham, Margaret Jones, Jonathan Kerry, Samuel McBratney, Joanna Thornton, Norman Wallwork and Pat Watson.

Discussion question: Paragraph 14 suggests a way of doing theology that is characteristically Methodist. Do you recognise this description? What are the advantages and disadvantages of doing theology this way?

C FOUR 'SNAPSHOTS' OF METHODIST COMMUNION SERVICES

19
In order to set the scene, we offer the following snapshots as examples of ways in which contemporary British Methodists celebrate Holy Communion. They are composite pictures, *not* caricatures, drawn from the research carried out by the working party, and in that sense are 'realistic'. They illustrate something of the considerable local variety in our Church.

20
At Woodlands Methodist Chapel, deep in the countryside, there is a Communion Service once a quarter. The minister has pastoral charge of eight other churches, so this is his only appointment here this quarter. The congregation is small, eight to twelve in number, all female and all senior citizens. The Communion Steward dices the slice of white bread into small cubes and pours the red grape juice into individual glasses. She directs the members up to the rail where they all kneel together to receive the elements, before being dismissed with a text of scripture or a short prayer. The Woodlands congregation likes to use the 1975 *Methodist Service Book* (from section B12), because "that's what we're used to". The minister wears a dark suit and clerical collar to lead the service. After worship, the remaining juice is poured back into the bottle and the bread put out for the birds.

21
At High Street Methodist Church, in the suburbs, there is a Service of Holy Communion once a month on a Sunday morning. The congregation comprises about 100 adults and 20 children. It is a multi-racial congregation, about half the membership is white, and half black. The children meet in Junior Church groups until near the end of the service, when they join their families in church for Communion. The minister has visited Junior Church to talk to the children about Communion. She has also consulted with parents about children receiving Communion. Any child or adult who wishes to receive is able to. The full service is from the *Methodist Worship Book*. The Peace is shared with much hugging and kissing, although this is not appreciated by everyone. The non-alcoholic Communion wine is poured into individual glasses and pieces of bread are broken from a roll. The Communion Stewards carry the elements to the congregation and the plates of bread and the trays of glasses are passed along the pews.

22

At Christchurch Methodist Church, in the centre of a market town, a small group of mainly younger people, drawn from around the circuit, meets for a monthly service of 'Contemporary Worship'. This always includes an informal celebration of Holy Communion. Liturgies from various sources are used (including Iona, Taizé and the St. Hilda Community) and worship songs, accompanied by a flautist, generally replace traditional hymns. The congregation sits in a circle, around a table on which is placed a candle, a chalice (containing non-alcoholic wine) and a home-baked loaf. The presiding minister, wearing a pectoral cross over a sweater, remains seated in the circle and the members of the congregation serve each other with the bread and wine. There is a period of open prayer in which personal and national concerns are shared, silence is observed and the laying-on of hands is offered to those who wish to receive it.

23

In St. John's Anglican-Methodist Local Ecumenical Partnership (LEP) the clergy of both denominations wear white cassock-albs with the appropriate seasonal stoles. At major festivals they concelebrate, using the denominational rites alternately. The presiding ministers face the congregation from behind the altar: 'altar' and, to a lesser extent, 'Eucharist' are words which now come fairly readily to Methodist lips here. There are two candles on the table and a chalice that is used at Methodist services for those involved in the distribution. The congregation leaves the rail in a continuous flow. The choir sings hymns or an anthem during the reception. Children are welcome to receive a blessing; the ecumenical Church Council continues to discuss the propriety of children receiving the elements. After the service, a few people receive the consecrated elements in their own homes. The remaining bread or wafers and wine are quietly consumed in the vestry.

Discussion question: Do any of these snapshots reflect the position in your church? If not, what would a snapshot of your church look like?

D A SURVEY OF CURRENT PRACTICE AND BELIEFS IN THE METHODIST CHURCH

(i) Background

24
The Working Party understood its task to be to report on Methodist belief and practice not only from the point of view of Methodist scholarship and official statements but also from the perspective of 'ordinary' Methodists. This approach was not adopted out of populism or a desire to replace rigorous theology, but from the fundamental understandings of the way that Methodists do theology, outlined in Section 2 above. For these reasons, it was decided to conduct a survey to investigate what Methodists believe and do about Holy Communion.

25
The next decision concerned the methodology of the survey. This was again informed by the relationship between the connexional and the local in Methodist theology and practice. The need to give weight both to connexional policies and to local variations led us to recognise the need for a survey. A statistically significant survey of a very large or random sample would have been informative but might, by its very existence, be counter-productive, suggesting that what is more prevalent is somehow more acceptable. The Working Party therefore decided to conduct a purely descriptive survey. We simply needed to test the perception that there is great variety of practice around Holy Communion in Methodism, and to try to find out why.

26
For ease and economy a questionnaire was distributed at the Huddersfield Conference in 2000. Every member of the Conference, together with ordinands and overseas representatives, was given three copies of the survey questionnaire. They were asked to fill in one copy themselves and pass on the others to people in their home setting, although this request was not universally carried out. 1350 questionnaires were sent out through Conference. The survey was also distributed through one District Synod and sent to individuals who requested it. This gave a good geographical spread, but it meant that the survey was not strictly representative of Methodism as a whole. In particular, the proportion of presbyters and deacons was higher than in the Church at large.

27

In addition, churches and circuits were invited (through the *Methodist Recorder* and the *Conference Bulletin*) to respond with more extended comments. 81 submissions were received, many of them substantial, and this material generally supported the evidence of the survey. It is quoted where appropriate in what follows – as indicated by the use of italics.

28

This survey illustrates some of the variety that exists in what Methodists believe and do about Holy Communion. Within the non-random and to some extent self-selected constituency there are clear trends and clusters: readers of the Report must use their own judgement in assessing how representative these are (more detailed analysis is available on request). The findings of the survey are offered as a description of one, not untypical section of Methodism against which experience and practice may be examined and questioned. Within the survey constituency there are valid comparisons to be made which throw up interesting insights. There is, for example, the difference between the beliefs and practices of presbyters, deacons and lay people. These will be examined as the survey is presented.

(ii) The findings of the survey

(Note: the fifteen numbered questions in the survey are quoted in **orange bold***)*

29

Question 1 Who are you?

429 questionnaires were returned altogether. The response rate (30%) is within normal limits for this type of survey, although it must be remembered that those for whom Holy Communion is too unimportant to rate a reply may have excluded themselves. All responses were anonymous and were not located geographically. 30% of replies were from British presbyters, 2% from overseas presbyters, 2% from British deacons and 66% from British lay people. Respondents were asked to reply for the church where they worshipped or (in the case of presbyters) presided at Communion most often.

30

Question 2 What do you call the service we are talking about?

As soon as the Working Party began discussions it became clear that Methodists use several different names for the sacrament in question. The name used may reflect

something of the theology of the individual or the community to which they belong. Survey respondents were most likely to call it 'Communion' and 'Holy Communion'. Presbyters were more likely than lay people to say 'Holy Communion' and far more likely to say 'Eucharist', although numbers were small. Only a few of them would say 'The Lord's Supper' (despite its use in official documents and liturgy) and 'The Sacrament' (even though this, or the symbol 'S', is commonly used on circuit plans), but while presbyters were in line with others on use of 'The Lord's Supper', no presbyter reported using 'The Sacrament'.

31
Individuals do not necessarily use the name that is used in the congregation to which they belong: more congregations than individuals were reported to use 'The Sacrament' as their preferred name, while fewer used 'The Eucharist', and of these 7 were Local Ecumenical Partnerships; only one was a British Methodist church alone.

32
Question 3 How often is Holy Communion celebrated as a Sunday service?

'Once a month' or 'less than once a week but more than once a month' were by far the most common frequencies for Sunday celebrations, accounting between them for nearly 90% of responses. More frequent celebrations were very uncommon. 5% reported 'less than once a month'.

33
Question 3a Would you like to see any changes, and if so, why?

A few people expressed the opinion that the service would be devalued or lose its special character if it were celebrated 'too often'. On the other hand, 16% of respondents said that they would like more frequent celebrations of Communion. Where reasons were given these focused on the 'essential' or 'central' nature of the sacrament. It is the *'equipping and focus of sacramental lifestyle'*, *'essential for building up the faith and fellowship'*, enabling people *'to relate to each other and their Christian origins'* and to the wider Church.

34
In response to this question, as to all the questions about change, presbyters were far more likely to express a preference.

35

Question 4 **How often is Holy Communion celebrated in the church building on other occasions (e.g. midweek)?**

In the great majority of cases (72%) this was 'less than once a month', sometimes amplified as meaning 'never' or 'at Christmas and Maundy Thursday'.

36

Question 4a **Would you like to see any changes, and if so, why?**

Unsurprisingly, those churches that had the least frequent midweek Communions produced the greatest desire for more. Overall nearly a quarter of respondents would like more frequent midweek Communion (no one requested less frequent). Reasons for wanting change clustered around four main themes: people's lifestyles, in terms both of work and church commitments, making Sundays problematic; the possibility of appealing to particular groups such as young parents, elderly or those attending a shoppers' service; building up fellowship with one another; the development of communion with God. *'To develop mystery and faith in daily discipleship.'*

37

Question 5 **In what form is the bread when it is placed on the table?**

Nearly half the respondents reported *'a whole roll, loaf or slice'* and a further 40% *'cut into small pieces with a roll or slice to be broken in the service'*. Most of the remainder reported the use of bread *'all cut into small pieces'*. There would thus seem to be widespread use within the survey group of the symbolism of fraction (breaking the bread in the course of the service).

38

Question 5a **Would you like to see any changes, and if so, why?**

There was a clear preference for a whole roll, stronger among presbyters. *'Dry bits of Mother's Pride is not my sense of the body of Christ.' 'A slice is part of something else and seems disrespectful and too ordinary.' 'God never serves us stale bread.'* Some responses gave sidelights on the importance (in terms both of spirituality and power relationships) of the practicalities of Holy Communion. Two lay people felt it important to mention the problems caused by the minister breaking off a piece that is too big for them to eat decorously. A minister would prefer a whole roll but *'recognises the care on the part of the Communion Stewards in preparing bread*

according to their tradition', while a layperson notes that *'ministers seem to have preferences'.* Otherwise the reasons for wanting change centred on the symbolism of one loaf, primarily as symbolising fellowship, breaking and generosity.

39

Question 6 What kind of 'wine' is used?

Of the 6 respondents who reported the use of alcoholic wine, 4 were in LEPs and one outside Great Britain. 79% reported the use of non-alcoholic Communion 'wine' containing grape juice and 15% (63 responses) 'other', divided roughly equally between grape juice, raisin flavoured or blackcurrant cordial (and one mead!).

40

Question 6a Would you like to see any changes, and if so, why?

This question attracted the greatest number of responses specifically saying 'no change': this indicates a strong commitment to the use of non-alcoholic 'wine'. This practice is, of course currently required by Standing Orders and was confirmed by the Conference only recently. Those expressing a desire for change were generally moving in the direction of greater authenticity; from blackcurrant cordial to non-alcoholic wine, from *'phoney wine'* to grape juice. Taste was also a significant factor. A few respondents would prefer alcoholic wine, mainly for reasons of authenticity. Presbyters were slightly more likely than lay people to want all these changes.

41

Question 7 Is a chalice or common cup placed on the table?

Roughly two-thirds of respondents reported having a chalice on the table. Wine was put in this chalice in most cases. When we were told who drank from a chalice on the table, it was most likely to be 'the presiding minister and those assisting her/him', followed by 'no-one' then 'the presiding minister' and 'everyone who communicates'.

42

Question 7a Would you like to see any changes, and if so, why?

A few lay people, but no presbyters, specifically expressed a preference for individual glasses, giving hygiene as the reason very occasionally. Other responses received

from circuits, on the other hand, indicated considerable concern with hygiene. *'The common cup is an artificial attempt to demonstrate unity (which) resides in the fellowship, including Christ.'* Nearly a quarter of respondents stated a preference for all to share one cup, mainly on grounds of unity, sharing, authenticity and symbolism. *'Individual glasses are prissy and an over-privatisation of Communion.'* A very few respondents saw the practice of the minister alone drinking from the chalice as elitist. *'It's the Lord's table. No one is in charge.'* Presbyters were markedly more in favour of a common cup but not necessarily for all to drink: they were more likely to want change in situations where a common cup was never used, but it was only lay people who asked that all should drink from the cup when one was placed on the table but not used by all.

43

Question 8 How are the bread and wine distributed?

The traditional method of distribution 'by tables' proved to be by far the most common, either alone or in combination with other methods. In most Methodist churches the worshippers communicate by kneeling at the Communion rail. They arrive and leave the table in groups (this sometimes described as 'by tables'), thus communicating in the 18th century Anglican style, but a custom now peculiar to the Methodist tradition. The continuous method of distribution was the next most common, although not often the only method used. A few churches reported having the elements brought round, although in most cases other methods of distribution were also used from time to time. Even fewer churches reported having the elements passed round, and this was only at some services.

44

Question 8a Would you like to see any changes and, if so, why?

Of those who expressed a preference for 'tables', most did so on grounds of dignity and less hurry. *'Coming forward and being blessed and dismissed is the most important part of the service.'* Of those who expressed a preference for continuous distribution, a third mentioned the time factor, while a very few found it more expressive of unity. Presbyters were in general more eager than lay people to change methods of distribution, particularly away from 'tables' and having the elements brought round. Responses to this question generally highlighted issues about time, dignity, the involvement of all who are present and the needs of the elderly.

45

Question 9 What happens to the bread and wine left over after the service?

Nearly one-fifth of respondents reported that the bread and wine were consumed, either by those who had distributed or by the Communion Stewards. In all other cases the more usual Methodist ways of disposal were used. Putting the wine back in the bottle and the bread out for the birds ('*they are God's creatures*') were the most common.

46

Question 9a Would you like to see any changes and, if so, why?

A small number expressed a preference for more dignified or reverent means of disposal, '*out of respect and love for the sacrifice made.*' There was hardly any reference to ecumenical sensibilities. Those who wanted change were nearly all asking for more reverent means of disposal. Presbyters were more than twice as likely as lay people to want such change.

47

Question 10 What forms of service are currently used?

Responses to this question showed a good deal of variety as well as widespread use of the 1999 *Methodist Worship Book (MWB)*. Use of the 1936 Book of Offices was reported by a very few, in most cases used 'occasionally'. Less than 10% of respondents reported using the 1975 *Methodist Service Book (MSB)* 'always'. Among the great majority who reported using *MWB* the most common patterns were to use either the whole service or part of it 'sometimes'. Over a quarter of respondents reported the use of *MWB* services 'always', either whole or in part. Those using *MWB* in part were more likely than those using whole services to use 'other' material as well. Nearly half reported the use of 'other' material 'occasionally' or 'sometimes'. Frustratingly, not many specified what kind of 'other', although a few mentioned Iona or extempore forms.

48

Question 10a Would you like to see any changes and, if so, why?

Some people expressed a preference for *MWB*, usually on the grounds of liking the variety of Communion service orders. '*It makes people think.*' '*It prevents force of habit.*'

A few liked the dignity of *MWB.'I have more regard for a set order – not made up liturgy with lots of hugging.'* Some mentioned particular elements of the service: the Creed, the Peace, and the Prayer of Humble Access. Concerns were expressed about formal or 'churchy' language, in a few cases for the sake of *'those not used to Church language.'* Some found too many words oppressive and asked for more space and silence.

49
Variety was also given as a reason for using 'other' material. A few people, on the other hand, expressed the view that there was too much variety. *'Congregations need to feel comfortable.'* Some people expressed a preference for *'the practice where no book is used and the minister takes the service in his* (sic) *own words'.* Most of those advocating more extempore liturgy were concerned with the distraction of following or holding the book, the difficulty of following rubrics, the danger of complacency and, in one case, the desire to have Communion services *'built around other gospel stories than the Last Supper.'*

50
Question 11 Do other people assist the presiding minister at a service which includes Holy Communion?

Responses to this question indicated that it was very common for people other than the minister to read from Scripture ('always' in nearly half of cases) and lead prayers, both intercessions and other prayers (rarely 'always' but either 'occasionally' or 'sometimes' in well over half of cases). Assisting with the distribution of the bread and wine was reported by a third of respondents 'occasionally' or 'sometimes' and a further third 'always'. Those who assisted were most likely to be a Communion Steward or Local Preacher, followed by a Church Steward, another minister and then a lay worker, unspecified other and deacon.

51
Question 11a Would you like to see any changes and, if so, why?

The practice of lay people assisting with the distribution of Communion was clearly widespread within the survey group. But there was also evidence of confusion and misunderstanding about what is involved. Those who wanted change were mainly looking for more involvement of lay people. For some this was simply a question of equality. *'Anyone who loves the Lord should be able to help.' 'We are all servants*

of God, so I feel it's a great privilege and more people should try it.' For others it was *'a symbol that the Sacrament is something that we are all sharing together, not something that is being done to us.'* For another small group it was important that those assisting should be authorised by the congregation or the church or in some way seen to be representative of it. *'A person who emerges as someone whom everyone respects and reveres.' 'From recognised roles and with some awareness/training.'* Lack of representative roles could lead to an unhelpful emphasis on personal qualities: *'some have told me, when approached, that they are 'not worthy' ... the question can become divisive.'* Some comments revealed confusion between presiding at Communion and distributing the bread and wine, and the significance of both. *'More involvement of lay non-leaders (would) underline (the) priesthood of all believers.' 'I would prefer ordained ministers to distribute the bread and wine always ... If we are all to be regarded as equal in the Communion service why do ministers have to be ordained?'* Others showed a lack of information: *'As Steward and senior Steward I didn't know I would be allowed to assist. I thought you had to be a Local Preacher.'*

52

Question 12 Are there occasions when your congregation would like to have a Communion service but is unable to do so because a minister is not available (e.g. at festival seasons)?

Just over a quarter of respondents answered "Yes" to this question. The most common reason given was 'not enough ministers', but reasons connected with bad planning were also given.

53

Question 12a What would you regard as the best solution to this problem?

A wide variety of solutions was suggested. Some respondents saw the possibility of changing service times, encouraging congregations to come together or sharing with other denominations. Some felt that there could be better use of ministers, including supernumeraries and ministers of other denominations. Among those who advocated some kind of authorisation there was a variety of proposals. Stewards, Local Preachers, Worship Leaders, deacons, Lay Workers, probationers and Communion Stewards were all mentioned, together with 'ordinary' or 'competent' lay people or those 'of good standing'. Underlying these suggestions may be discerned a

variety of theological ideas. Some discerned a need for training ('competence' was also mentioned). Some emphasised prayerful discernment. Some suggested appointment by the Circuit, others by the congregation. Some looked for seniority, good standing or those well established in an office, others for all those in a category (such as Local Preacher) to be eligible. No one specifically mentioned authorisation by the Conference.

54

Question 13 Are there any circumstances in which it would not be appropriate for someone to receive the bread and wine?

Note: The mere asking of this question, and the next two, presupposes to some extent that 'there is a case to answer'. The underlying issues were selected as important following some preliminary conversations with a range of individuals and groups about the sort of questions that might be asked in the survey.

Most respondents felt that there should, in general, be no bar to people receiving the bread and wine. Those who answered "yes" to this question (clearly a minority) cited a number of different possible circumstances. The reasons most often mentioned were unresolved conflict, lack of penitence or blatant insincerity; public scandal *("local rogues")*; very young children, or children whose parents had not given permission; the ignorant or "unchurched".

55

Many felt that the decision whether or not to receive the elements should be a personal one, left to the conscience of the individual. Very little mention was made of Church discipline, although a few suggested that if someone had been expelled from membership for disciplinary reasons, they should be excluded. One respondent wrote of the danger of "abuse of the privilege" with regard to Communion, and another suggested that it should be up to the minister to decide.

56

Question 14 How important is Holy Communion to you? Please give your reasons.

The majority of respondents wrote that Holy Communion is important to them, and many wrote that it is either *"very"* or *"extremely"* important. Communion was described as *"vital"*, *"essential"*, *"a central building block"* or the *"supreme act of*

worship". A significant minority, however, expressed the view that, whilst it is important, it is no more so than other acts or aspects of worship: *"I could survive without it"*. A few suggested that its specialness lies in its relative rarity and believe it to be devalued by over-frequent celebration.

57
Many reasons for regarding Communion as important were given. Grouped and listed roughly in order of popularity, the most common were:

- the awareness of the death/sacrifice of Christ – *"what Christ has done for me"* – and the forgiveness of sins; a reminder of Christ's self-giving, his blood *"shed for me personally"*, so that I might have eternal life; God's gift to us; celebration of the Easter faith
- the sense of fellowship with those sharing with us, but also with Christians around the world and in a continuing link going back through history to the experience of the first disciples at the Last Supper; the sense of being *"Christ's body"*; being united *"regardless of status"*; the family of the Lord is together, entering into Christ's passion; Christ creates community
- obedience to Christ; Christ requested that we should receive; Communion was instituted by Jesus; Communion is *"a symbolic re-enactment of the Last Supper"*
- foretaste of the heavenly banquet; a vision of sharing in the kingdom yet to come
- the opportunity for renewal, *"forgiveness of sins"*, *"healing"* and *"peace"*; a fresh start is given; we are sent out into the world with *"strengthening of the power to love and serve"*; we find spiritual strength and nourishment
- we come to Christ in a uniquely *"personal way"*; we are *"face to face with the Lord"*
- the sense of history and tradition; *"... it has been important to the Church as a whole over the centuries"*
- engages all five senses; it is *"holistic"* and with sign and symbol *"gets beyond our obsession with words"*; it communicates to us at many different levels
- gives opportunity for reflection and helps us find inner peace; *"gives a standard of holiness"*
- a central aspect of the call to, and vital part of, ministry; an extension of pastoral care; it *"sustains, cleanses and energises for ministry"* and strengthens faith; the *"unique pastoral relationship"* between minister and congregation is highlighted during distribution.

58

Question 15 **Do you believe or feel that Christ is present at the Lord's Supper in a unique or special way? Please give your reasons.**

A clear majority answered "Yes" to this question. Some added that Christ's presence is also mediated through other services. Many of the answers suggest that the respondents feel that Christ's presence is experienced in a "special" rather than "unique" way at the Lord's Supper, but these words mean different things to different people, are frequently confused, or are taken to be identical in meaning. A few people answered with a definite "No", and a few were ambiguous, saying "Sometimes", "Maybe" or "Yes and no". A bewildering variety of reasons was expressed.

59

Amongst the answers of those who did not believe, or who were cautious about the notion of the presence of Christ being either uniquely or specially present were the following (listed in no particular order):

- Christ is present in all times and places; *"he is everywhere the same. It is how much we are tuned in"*; it is our perception of him that changes
- we mustn't restrict Christ's presence, or *"overstate"* the uniqueness of the sacrament
- it depends on the minister taking the service, or the style of the service; *"presbyters have no power to summon Christ's presence"*
- Christ is not localised in the elements
- He isn't specially present but we feel closer and more receptive
- *"Christ's presence is 'real' wherever his people meet in his name"*.

60

The responses of the majority, who believed that Christ is present in a special or unique way, were also many and varied, and included the following (similar points from different respondents have been grouped together):

- the elements are *"physical representations of Christ offered to each individual and taken and held by each individual"*; *"Bread and wine become for us the body and blood of Christ"*

- Christ promised we would receive, and that he would be present, through the Holy Spirit ... Jesus is there in the Holy Spirit; it is a spiritual presence
- Christ invites to, and presides at, his table; he is the host ... he is present, just as he was at the Last Supper ... we are like the disciples
- *"He just fills my heart – inexplicable" ... "I just 'feel' him, like He's hugging me, holding me in his arms"*
- *"symbolism is a gateway to perception"*
- *"Jesus is present in the bread and wine – a great mystery; Jesus is there for me"*
- Christ is *"both priest and victim"*
- Communion is a foretaste of the heavenly banquet
- *"Communion gives me a closer, one-to-one relationship"*
- Christ is present in the body of believers, gathered together.

61
Only six or seven respondents used the phrase *"the real presence"*, and a few stated their *"clear rejection of the doctrine of transubstantiation"*. There was a general lack of emphasis on the bread and wine as vehicles of Christ's presence. A small number commented in their response to this question that they had made a personal commitment to Christ through, or during a Communion service.

62
In conclusion, it can be observed that there are many and various views about Communion expressed in the survey. Most respondents believed that Communion should be open to all, and that the decision whether or not to receive should be made by each individual. The majority said that Communion was important to them, and that they believed that Christ was present in a special way in the Communion, though not necessarily *"uniquely"* present. For many, Communion was tremendously important for their personal faith, but within this the corporate dimension of Communion was felt to be extremely important. We conclude that Methodists gain personal strength from this sacrament, but they wish to receive it together: many respondents wrote of the power of Communion to unite the people of Christ.

Discussion questions: In what ways does practice in your church reflect the responses to the questionnaire? What do you find helpful? Does anything surprise you? What changes would you like to see in practice in your church? And why?

Do you agree with the views given in answer to questions 14 and 15?

E OTHER CHARACTERISTIC FEATURES OF COMMUNION IN THE METHODIST CHURCH

(i) Holy Communion liturgies

63

Prior to the publication of the 1975 *Methodist Service Book (MSB)*, Methodist liturgical provision for Holy Communion was found in the 1936 *Book of Offices*, with two forms. The first was essentially that of the 1662 *Book of Common Prayer*. The second, 'alternative' form, was shorter and attempted to reflect the written forms of the non-Wesleyan traditions, although in practice many of them had been rather more informal. The *MSB* 'Sunday Service' provided for the first time a service in contemporary language and, in its name, signalled the closer integration of Holy Communion into the 'mainstream' of Methodist worship, rather than being very often an 'optional extra' for the very committed. The newer liturgy soon established its dominance over earlier forms and assisted the growth in frequency with which Communion was now being celebrated in our churches.

64

This very 'success', together with rapid developments in liturgical language in other traditions and the emergence of new theological concerns, notably that of inclusive language, contributed to a movement for further development, and the eventual appearance of the 1999 *Methodist Worship Book (MWB)*. In its eucharistic provision, *MWB* offers eight full orders, following the main seasons and festivals of the Christian year as well as 'Ordinary Seasons', not to mention seven further Communion orders for particular occasions such as Holy Week, Covenant, Marriage, Healing and Ordination services. Each of these orders has a distinctive 'feel', appropriate to the occasion, time of year or reflecting different emphases. There is much greater use of signs and symbols and a wider variety of poetic imagery, although many of these features are offered as suggestions rather than being in any sense mandatory, thus reflecting the variety of liturgical preference within the Church today.

65

To highlight the chief changes introduced with *MWB* is perhaps to play down the significant continuities in style and theology compared with its predecessors and many of the liturgies currently emerging in other denominations. However,

we may note a few features briefly:

- the use of a stronger 'epiclesis' (invocation of the Holy Spirit) in the eucharistic prayers
- the re-introduction of the 'Prayer of Humble Access' in a version close to Cranmer's 16th century original, alongside the *MSB* text, which had gained considerable popularity
- reinstatement of the traditional language of 'angels and archangels' rather than simply 'the company of heaven'
- a wider use of 'feminine' imagery throughout and a eucharistic prayer addressed to 'God our Father *and our Mother*', included after vigorous debate
- material drawn from a wide range of other Christian traditions
- the inclusion of familiar music in one of the orders of service for Communion.

66
However, despite the 'success' of *MWB* (almost 250,000 copies sold) and the continuing use of *MSB* in many places and the 1936 service in a few, these 'official' liturgies have never been exclusive of all others. Indeed, it would appear that there is even greater variety in liturgical use today than ever before. Extensive use is made of liturgies from such sources as the Iona Community, contemporary Christian writers and other denominations, and many congregations use extempore and 'home grown' liturgies, at least on some occasions. The ready availability of facilities for local reproduction of printed material has facilitated these developments. Such variety and creativity is a witness to the vibrant eucharistic life of Methodist Churches, and the continued interest in exploring the many theological riches of this sacrament. It is also in keeping with the status of the liturgies authorised by the Conference as a standard for Methodist worship: 'these forms are not intended to curb creative freedom, but rather to provide norms for its guidance.' (*Preface to MSB, quoted in preface to MWB*). *MWB* offers a section of guidance for ordering a service of Holy Communion on occasions when the full liturgies are not used.

67
It is also important to note traditions of 'informal' and 'extempore' observance of Communion. This may take the form of a 'minimalist' liturgy, and/or eschew written forms for a freer expression of thanksgiving and remembrance. One common pattern, differing from that in the 'authorised' liturgies, and akin to that of some 'Reformed'

Churches, is that of 'Narrative of Institution' (typically a reading of the account of the Last Supper in 1 Corinthians 11), followed by prayers of intercession and then the Sharing of the Bread and Wine.

68
However, it is undoubtedly the case that in Methodism, the publication of a new book of liturgies (as of a hymn book) is a significant event, and a spirit of connexionalism is reinforced, as the new material becomes, in most places, the 'norm'.

Discussion questions: Read alongside this section of the report the introduction to the Holy Communion services on pages 114-115 of the Methodist Worship Book and the guidance on pages 221-222 of MWB. What do you welcome in the provision for Holy Communion in MWB? Does it provide enough variety or too much?

Bearing in mind what is said in the preface to MWB (page viii) about all the services in that book being intended as norms for guidance rather than restrictions on creative freedom, is enough use made of 'creative freedom' when Holy Communion is celebrated in your church?

(ii) Hymnody and Holy Communion

69
Hymns are important to Methodists at Holy Communion, as elsewhere in their worship. The increased importance of Holy Communion in Methodist consciousness and worship is underlined by the increased provision, as compared with earlier hymnals, of hymns suitable for Holy Communion in *Hymns & Psalms*. It contains 39 hymns in the section on the Lord's Supper as against 18 in the 1933 *Methodist Hymn Book*.

70
The hymns in total represent a blend of traditional and contemporary. As well as eucharistic hymns by the Wesleys and 'traditional' writers, there are also a translation of part of the 'eucharistic' prayer from the *Didache* and 20th century hymns by Fred Pratt Green, Fred Kaan, Brian Wren and Patrick Appleford. These also stress the dynamic nature of the encounter of the living Christ with his people at the Lord's Supper.

71
Taking the eucharistic hymns in *HP* as a whole, one can discern certain recurrent themes. There is a strong emphasis upon celebration, set in the very first hymn, 592 and maintained in a variety of ways in others e.g. 606, 609, 610 (with a more individual emphasis). Another emphasis is upon eschatological expectation and longing for the fulfilment of the experience to which Holy Communion points e.g. 598, 600, 603. Many hymns stress the spiritual nourishment received at Holy Communion, e.g. 595, 604, 608, 611, 613, 620. Several hymns stress the way in which Holy Communion enhances and deepens the unity and fellowship of the Church. The best two examples of this are to be found at 612, 'Jesus invites His saints' and 622, 'See where our great high priest'. Dedication, and inspiration to dedication are emphasised in several hymns e.g. 594 and 595.

72
It is traditional, at least in some circles in Methodism, to ascribe great importance to the 166 *'Hymns on the Lord's Supper'*, written by the Wesley brothers. What is not simple to ascertain is the degree to which they have been used and their theology 'received' by the Methodist people in succeeding generations. This collection of hymns is not readily accessible to the 'ordinary' Methodist. A few, certainly, have appeared in successive official Methodist hymnals. Only one, 'Victim Divine, Thy grace we claim', appeared in the last two Wesleyan books, of 1877 and 1904, and the two books of reunited Methodism 1933 and 1983. In practice, the hymns of the Wesleys do not represent the contemporary understanding and piety of many Methodists.

73
Nevertheless, if Methodism is to be faithful to the obligation to wrestle with its tradition, perhaps it should continue to take account of the hymns that undoubtedly present a very rich and nuanced understanding of Holy Communion. The hymns, mainly written by Charles, are arranged in six sections, viz.- 'As it is a memorial of the sufferings of Christ', 'As it is a sign and a means of grace', 'The sacrament as a pledge of heaven', 'The Holy Eucharist as it implies a sacrifice', 'Concerning the sacrifice of our persons' and 'After the sacrament'. The comprehensiveness of their coverage anticipates much that was to become commonplace in the Liturgical Movement and in contemporary ecumenical consensus on Holy Communion. Though only eight of the hymns are in the present *Hymns & Psalms*, they do reflect this comprehensiveness and richness, including, as they do, a hymn invoking the Holy Spirit (602), a hymn emphasising the eucharistic sacrifice (629), others reflecting the eschatological dimension of Holy Communion (e.g. 598, 614) and one

reflecting the intimate union of Christ and His people (622). A constant emphasis is upon the joyful mystery of Holy Communion in such couplets as:

'He bids us eat and drink
Imperishable food'.

or

'Who Thy mysterious supper share.
Here at thy table fed'
(*HP* 614)

74

The essential feature of the eucharistic piety of the Wesley's with which contemporary Christians of all denominations would do well to engage, is its sense of doxological awe and wonder, as seen in such verses as:

O, the depth of love divine,
the unfathomable grace!
Who shall say how bread and wine
God into man (*sic*) conveys!

and

Let us taste the heavenly powers,
Lord we ask for nothing more.
Thine to bless, 'tis only ours
To wonder and adore'.

and

Angels round our altars bend
To search it out in vain.

75

The eucharistic hymns of the Wesleys focus on the union of Christ with His people at the Lord's Supper. Some of their phraseology may be felt problematic for the present generation, but a vital dimension of eucharistic spirituality might be lost were they to fall completely out of use. It could be argued that Methodism has a duty to commend their appreciation to the wider Christian world.

Discussion question: Read carefully the hymns mentioned in this section and discuss your reactions to them.

(iii) Communion and conversion

76

In the early days of Methodism, members of the societies were expected to continue to attend the parish church to receive Communion, so questions about admission did not immediately arise. When they did, as in so many other matters of Church order, John Wesley was so committed to what he believed to be the pattern of the primitive Church that he regarded baptism as a sufficient qualification for admission to Communion. Indeed, he completely omitted the rite of confirmation from his *Sunday Service* revision of the Book of Common Prayer. In his abridgement of his father's *Short Discourse of Baptism*, which Wesley published in 1756, he declared baptism to be the initiatory sacrament of entry into the covenant, of entry into the Church and of incorporation into Christ. Neither of the Wesley brothers ever wrote anything about confirmation. Charles Wesley was in the habit of baptising those who became believers before admitting them to the Lord's Supper. During the Methodist revival John Wesley welcomed English dissenters to Communion on the assumption that they had been baptised.

77

John Wesley urged those who believed that Christ had died for them to eat of the bread and drink of the cup at the Lord's Table. Furthermore, from the 1740s he stood out against those who took the view that the Lord's Supper was only a 'confirming ordinance' leading from confessing faith to fullness of faith. On the grounds of experience Wesley declared that there were those who owed the very beginning of their conversion to God to what God had worked in them at the Lord's Supper: it was a 'converting ordinance'. The teaching of the Wesleys was that Communion could lead a genuine seeker first to find Christ, then to be justified by believing faith and finally through constant attendance at the Lord's Supper and the other means of grace to reach a state of scriptural holiness and entire sanctification in heart and life, having been made perfect in love. The Lord's Supper was ordained by God as a means of conveying 'preventing (i.e. prevenient), justifying or sanctifying grace'.

78

In their joint manifesto *Hymns on the Lord's Supper (1745)* the Wesleys placed a huge emphasis on sinners finding salvation at the Table of the Lord. The Lord's Table in early Methodism was however 'fenced' by the dual requirement of evidence of fleeing from sin and a genuine seeking after Christ and in addition a 'class ticket' or 'Communion note' from the Wesleys themselves or from one of their Assistants. John Wesley stated emphatically 'no fitness is required at the time of communicating, but a sense of utter

sinfulness and helplessness'. The Lord's Supper was open to all *bona fide* seekers however frail their hold upon the faith. Some ten years into the Methodist revival the Wesleys were at pains to admit to Communion only those they knew to be seekers. 'Strangers' were not admitted to Communion without a 'ticket' from one of Wesley's assistants. Admission was by presentation to the Steward of a 'society ticket' or a 'band ticket' or a 'Communion ticket' or, in Scotland, 'a Communion token'. After 'morning prayer' or 'the preaching' those without admission tickets would leave.

79
In the early part of the nineteenth century both the Wesleyan and the Primitive Methodist traditions required a ticket or note of admission from those attending the Lord's Supper. The United Methodist Free Churches recognised at the Lord's Supper both their own 'sacramental members' who had a monthly Communion ticket and 'strangers' who would eventually be approached about becoming 'sacramental members'.

80
The Wesleyan Methodists lived with a dichotomy. On the one hand they never rescinded the rule that no one should partake of the sacrament unless they could present a class ticket or a quarterly note of admission. On the other hand, in practice, the Wesleyan Conference claimed no one had ever been denied the Lord's Supper if they did present themselves without a ticket! The present and almost universal Methodist custom of inviting to the Lord's Table 'all those who love the Lord Jesus Christ' (the so-called 'open table') is a phenomenon that developed in the twentieth century. The primary motive behind this practice is the belief that none should be prevented from finding and receiving the love and nourishment which Christ offers at his table. It enshrines Wesley's concept of the Lord's Supper as a 'converting ordinance' open to all 'seekers' and avoids deciding at each celebration who are 'members' and who are not. The 1975 *Methodist Service Book* tried to take a tighter view and indicated that only communicant members of other Churches, whose discipline so permitted, were welcome to receive Communion in Methodist congregations. Provision was made in the rubric for 'those who leave' to do so after the prayers of intercession, before the sharing of the Peace, reflecting the earlier custom that Holy Communion was, in practice, an observance only for the most committed, adult believers. The 2000 Conference, referring back to Guidelines about Children and Holy Communion issued in 1987, affirmed that those receiving Communion should, if not already baptized, be encouraged to be baptized – but acknowledged that this 'theological principle' was not widely adhered to.

81
Methodism came late to the idea of a liturgical act for making members. Young people were encouraged to see their becoming members as the occasion for starting to receive Communion. Ever since first using the term 'confirmation' in the mid-1960s, Methodism has been confused about the meaning and purpose of that rite. When Methodism moved to a position of inviting children to receive Holy Communion it was baptism, parental permission and catechesis that became the necessary or highly desirable criteria.

82
Both the Wesley brothers administered Communion to catechised children at their own Kingswood School near Bristol. John Wesley's journal implies that all he required of any child before giving them Communion was 'a sense of the pardoning love of God'. The *Methodist Service Book* expected children to come to the rail – but for a blessing rather than to receive the bread and wine. Clearly, the customary Methodist open invitation to Communion, to all who love the Lord Jesus Christ was not, in practice, intended to include children. But even this was an advance on the practice in most Methodist churches prior to this time, to celebrate Holy Communion as an 'add-on', after the main service was concluded – few children would have even been present in church, and could only speculate as to the mysteries hidden under the white Communion tablecloth. However, by 2000 British Methodism had undergone a major shift on the place of children at Holy Communion, as outlined below (see paragraphs 133-135).

(iv) Communion Stewards

83
The office of Communion Steward gives a distinctively Methodist flavour to the organisation of a Communion service. The office originated with the Poor Stewards of the Methodist societies: when the societies began to celebrate their own Communion services (especially after the Plan of Pacification of 1795) an offering was commonly taken for the relief of the poor. The existing Poor Stewards thus became responsible for the arrangements for the service. This dual responsibility is still enshrined in Standing Orders (SO 637). Communion Stewards are appointed by the Church Council to 'make provision for the proper celebration of the sacrament' and to be responsible for a separate collection, if one is taken, for the benevolence fund or other charitable purpose authorised by the Church Council. This degree and type of delegation, with the associated use of the term 'Steward', gives the office its Methodist

character. The (itinerant) minister has great influence but does not totally control the arrangements for Communion services.

84
This shared responsibility invests the office of Communion Steward with great dignity and significance although on one level the tasks are wholly practical. Communion Stewards are generally responsible for providing the bread and wine, setting the table, ushering communicants to the place of distribution and (usually) all aspects of clearing the table, as well as overseeing the care of the table linen. Conversation with Communion Stewards frequently reveals the spirit of humility, reverence and love in which the service is offered, and the joy of being at the heart of the liturgy in this supremely practical way.

85
Conversation, together with comments from the survey, also reveals the delicate balance of influence and expectation focused on the office. Communion Stewards may have their own traditions about the type of bread and wine used and the forms in which they are provided, while different ministers and members of the congregation may have other preferences. Members of the congregation are unlikely to question the Communion Stewards' practices; ministers may feel it would be insensitive or impolitic to do so. The disposal of the bread and wine is often the Communion Stewards' responsibility to the extent that others do not know how it is done. The task of 'directing the approach of communicants to the Lord's Table in an orderly and expeditious manner' (SO 637) is felt as a heavy burden by some Communion Stewards, due largely, it would seem, to the awareness of time pressures revealed by the survey.

(v) The setting of Holy Communion

86
In the latter part of the twentieth century, there was a renewed awareness among Methodists of the significance of how church architecture and furnishings both express and shape our faith. In *Groundwork of Worship and Preaching* (Epworth Press 1980, p.9ff.), Richard Jones describes different types of Methodist church buildings. In the first, (typically 19th century), the pulpit dominates, below which there is a small Communion table and rail. The architecture emphasises the importance of preaching rather than Communion. The second type (probably dating from around 1860 - 1900) is a grand, "parish church" style building, with transepts and a chancel. The

Communion table is raised on high, at the far end of the chancel, emphasising the transcendence and mystery of God. Another type is the multi-purpose hall (probably built between the 1930s and 1960s), with a sanctuary area at one end that is screened off, except on Sundays. Within the sanctuary area there is a pulpit to one side, a font and a small, central Communion table. The sanctuary area within a hall used for purposes other than worship suggests a belief in the presence of the Word and Sacraments in the midst of daily life, although the screening of the area suggests a separation of worship from daily life. The last of Jones' examples is a modern church building, with a pulpit or lectern to one side at the front of the worship area, and a central table, on a raised area, around which people will kneel to receive the elements. The centrality of the table reflects the increased awareness amongst many Methodist people of the importance of Communion.

87

Susan White (*Groundwork of Christian Worship*, Epworth Press 1997, p.77) observes that "... in the past half-century, important changes in Communion practice, in baptismal theology, in the role of music, and in our understanding of the nature and mission of the Christian community have shaped and reshaped the setting in which Christian worship now takes place". This can be seen in many churches where the Communion table, originally distant from the people, has been brought forward to a position of greater prominence within the worship area. Instead of people walking up the chancel towards the table, there is more of a feeling of being gathered around the table. In many churches the table was originally positioned against a wall, or at the base of a pulpit and, where space permits, the table has been drawn forward so the minister can preside from behind the table, facing the people. (See John Lampard, *It's More than Washing Glasses*, MPH 1987, p.7)

88

Methodists, always borrowers, have unashamedly begun to learn about the movement and shape of the liturgical year and its accompanying liturgies and customs from Churches where such traditions are much stronger. Banners and liturgical hangings have become widespread features of Methodist churches, evidence of a renewed appreciation of the visual dimension to worship. Sacramental stoles in traditional liturgical colours are increasingly being worn by ministers presiding at services of Holy Communion. Some ministers have sought a measure of ecumenical convergence in the wearing of a white cassock-alb, but others feel that more informal ways of celebrating Holy Communion should be led by people more informally dressed. In a pluralist age there is inevitably less uniformity and not a few

ministers have adopted individualistic and idiosyncratic forms of dress. A report on liturgical dress adopted by the Conference in 1987 gave some guidance on these matters, but there seems little prospect of universal agreement.

89
Another effect of liturgical renewal is seen in the 'art of presidency.' The older Anglican and Methodist practice was basically for the priest or minister simply to stand or kneel at one end of the table and 'read' the service. In Methodism it was not unknown for ministers to read the service facing the congregation with their backs to the elements. Sometimes, the presiding minister would 'take' the bread and the cup at the 'offertory' or during the words of institution (the 'manual acts') and sometimes, apart from the earlier removal of the upper cloth, during the Communion hymn, no attention was drawn to the elements at all until the moment they were required for distribution.

90
In more recent years presiding ministers have been introduced to a wider variety of possibilities. These include first, sitting near the table during the service (especially when others are taking part in the Ministry of the Word) as the visible 'president' of the service; secondly, standing behind a free-standing table facing the congregation during the Prayer of Thanksgiving; and thirdly, placing the book on the table so that the hands and arms are free and they can preside at the liturgy with simple actions rather than just reading from a book held in the hand. The overriding aim is to engage with the worshipping assembly in a corporate event. Some have argued that, like a good teacher, something of the professional actor in the presiding minister can help to 'lift' the whole drama of the eucharistic event 'off the page and into the life of the congregation'.

Discussion question: How important is the setting of Holy Communion to you? Is it helpful to think of a celebration of Holy Communion as 'drama'?

(vi) Observations from circuit plans

91
A statistical analysis of circuit plans undertaken by John Lenton (*Epworth Review*, October 2000) demonstrates that Methodists now celebrate Communion more frequently than previously. Using plans from circuits in various parts of England, from

the periods 1807-1926 (including examples from Wesleyan, Primitive and United circuits) and 1997-2000, the percentage of services that were marked as Holy Communion was calculated for each plan. It was shown that, in the earlier period, this percentage figure was 2.08%, compared to 20.31% for the more recent period.

92
A separate analysis of circuit plans was undertaken on behalf of the Working Party, looking at the years 1960-2000, and using similar methods, although drawing samples from a much smaller number of circuits. Although this survey was only partial, there was a clear indication that there had been an increase in the frequency of Communion services over the period. A sample of plans from four circuits in four different Districts from 1969 showed that 13.8% of services were Communions. Plans from the same circuits for 1999 showed that 16.6% of services were Communions.

93
The frequency and regularity of Communions on some plans was clearly affected by the preferences of the minister in pastoral charge, and would change with a change of minister. On some more recent plans, the figures were influenced by the presence of an Anglican/ Methodist LEP, with a weekly celebration of Communion.

(vii) Methodist scholars who have made a significant contribution to our understanding of Holy Communion

Space does not permit a full account of the writings of the many Methodist scholars who have contributed to the Church's thinking. The following summary is offered simply to indicate some of the most significant contributors and something of their thought.

94
Long before it was fashionable Adam Clarke (c.1760-1832) drew scholarly and original parallels between Passover and Communion and laid the foundations for work which reached its finest exposition in the writings of William Burt Pope (1822-1903). Pope wrote of Baptism and Lord's Supper as the Spirit's instruments in aiding and strengthening faith:'In the eucharistic commemoration (we obtain) all the benefits of the sacrifice'.

95
Joseph Agar Beet (1840-1924) set out a famous parallel between word and sacrament. 'Just as in the preached word and in the fullest sense (we have) the real and objective

presence of the crucified God ... So we need not hesitate to say, that in the same sense, we have his real presence in the Lord's Supper. To the eye of faith the symbols disappear and the infinite reality alone remains'. Charles Ryder Smith (1875-1956) in his *Sacramental Society* (1927) put forward the distinction later taken up with some force by Gordon Wakefield (1921 - 2000) that Methodist eucharistic theology and devotional practice revealed a profound distinction between 'sacramentalists' which Methodists undoubtedly were and 'sacerdotalists' which Methodists were undoubtedly not.

96
J. Ernest Rattenbury (1870-1963) developed Richard Watson's determination to find a Methodist understanding of Holy Communion based on the Wesleys themselves. Rattenbury insisted that in their devotion to the Lord's Supper the Wesleys' experience of 1738 simply set on fire the sacramental foundations already laid. The Lord's Supper became an instrument of the gospel. In *The Eucharistic Hymns of John and Charles Wesley* (1948) Rattenbury also brought to the fore the distinctive eucharistic theology of the Wesley brothers set out in *Hymns on the Lord's Supper* (1745). A vigorous critique of the Wesleys' slavish adherence to Dean Brevint and of Rattenbury's interpretation was supplied by Franz Hildebrandt (1909-1985) in *I Offered Christ: A Protestant Study of the Mass* (1967). Hildebrandt's interpretations were themselves overturned by Bishop Ole Borgen in *John Wesley and the Sacraments* (1974).

97
The eucharistic practice of Methodism was set out in two classic studies by John C. Bowmer (1911-2000), *The Sacrament of the Lord's Supper in Early Methodism* (1951) and a sequel covering the years 1792-1960. In 1962 in Dow Kirkpatrick's symposium on *The Doctrine of the Church* Raymond George (1912-1998) produced perhaps the finest of all reflections on the Wesleys and Holy Communion in which he concluded that *Hymns on the Lord's Supper (1745)* owed far more to Cyprian than to Augustine. 'In the Eucharist we are brought into the heavenly places and there is made present to us, the once for all sacrificial act of Christ.'

98
The most monumental piece of original twentieth century Methodist writing on Holy Communion was undoubtedly Geoffrey Wainwright (1939-) in his *Eucharist and Eschatology* (1971; re-issued, Epworth Press 2003) in which he could claim that 'not until the *Wesleys' Hymns on the Lord's Supper (1745)* did the Western Church achieve again the richness and appreciation of Holy Communion as a sign of the future banquet of the heavenly kingdom.'

(viii) 'Semi-official' Methodist publications

Methodist thinking and practice is influenced by resources such as those mentioned here which, whilst not having the formal authority of the Conference, have been published by connexional bodies.

99

There are a number of relatively recent publications that, whilst not actually sanctioned by the Conference, describe the Methodist Church and its history, theology and current practices. Many of these are published by the Methodist Publishing House (MPH), or the Epworth Press. Among the most recent is Michael Townsend's *The Sacraments* (Epworth Press 1999). Some of these publications illustrate something of Methodist belief and practice with regard to Communion. For example, the booklet *It's more than washing glasses* by John Lampard (MPH, 1987) describes the duties of a Communion Steward. The practicalities of the task are outlined, but the Communion Steward's role in enhancing the atmosphere "of something which is both holy and joyful" (p.19) is also stressed.

100

Discussions about children and Communion have produced a number of publications over the years, including *Children at Holy Communion. One Body With Him* (Peter Sulston and Leigh Pope, MDEY 1989). In this booklet the Lord's Supper is described as a "proclamation of the Gospel" and "a means of grace, God's sign to us of his love, the assurance that Christ who met and ministered to people in his earthly ministry, meets and ministers to his people now".

101

In Rupert Davies' *What Methodists Believe* (Epworth Press 1976, 1988) there is no sustained focus on the sacrament of Communion and no specifically Methodist beliefs or practices are highlighted. We are told, however, that "The Lord's Supper supplies the regular nourishment we need for sustaining our Christian life". Moreover, Jesus "can and does come to us to be the host at his supper as a living personal reality from whom we can receive once again his gift of himself..." (p. 42). He is the host and we are the guests. Through Communion "... The whole action of God in Christ for the salvation of mankind becomes ours in the present time" (p. 43).

102

A lack of direct focus on Communion is also found in Thomas Langford's *Methodist*

Theology, in the *Exploring Methodism* Series (Epworth Press 1998). References to the Lord's Supper in this book are generally confined to the discussion on events leading to the 1932 union and the debate on presidency (p.73f). With regard to presidency at the Lord's Supper, Langford comments that "The minister neither adds an essential element nor is the sacrament specifically activated by the minister's presence" (p.92). (This emphasis on the question of presidency reflects the emphasis found in Conference statements with regard to Communion.)

103
The leaflet *The Methodist Church, an introduction* (MPH 1998; part of a set of materials designed as an introduction to the Methodist Church) observes that Holy Communion is at the heart of our worship. Through Communion we remember the Last Supper, and receive the Holy Spirit into our lives. It says, "all that is wrong in our lives can be dealt with and we are given hope and strength".

(ix) Ecumenical and other experiences

104
Methodist appreciation of the breadth and variety of practice, spirituality and theology of Holy Communion has grown considerably over the last generation. Both wider travel and increased ecumenical co-operation and friendship across traditional denominational boundaries have contributed to this. A considerable number of Methodists have experience of the eucharistic worship of other traditions through Local Ecumenical Partnerships, shared worship and visits to other churches. The majority of our ministers are now trained alongside those of other denominations. There is also much 'informal ecumenism', as denominational allegiances become more fluid. Some have been considerably attracted to the eucharistic ethos of other Churches, both those with a more 'catholic' and 'liturgical' style and those in the simpler tradition common in the other Free Churches. Thus, for example, some Methodists have come to a more rounded appreciation of Holy Communion as making present sacramentally the great events of salvation. Others treasure the emphasis upon Holy Communion as a corporate act, vividly signified by such practices as all receiving the elements simultaneously in the pews or 'in the round'. In the latter case, the survival of some pre-Union practices from the smaller Methodist Churches has also played a role.

105
In some quarters, the influence of the avowedly ecumenical 'Iona' liturgies, with

their combination of tradition and modernity in structure, style and phraseology, has been profound. Some Methodists have been and continue to be influenced by traditions and practices that view every part of life as sacramental, for example the Society of Friends, with their emphasis upon every meal as an occasion for thanksgiving for all God's benefits.

106

One Bread, One Body (1998) is the Roman Catholic bishops' (of Britain and Ireland) teaching document on Holy Communion. Most ecumenical partners have expressed admiration of its clarity and the Anglican bishops acknowledged the general acceptability of much of its general teaching, although much of it would probably be put differently, but not contradictorily, by others. The one area which has caused particular controversy has been over the very restricted guidelines for eucharistic hospitality spelt out by the Roman Catholic bishops, which is felt by some to be a less than generous interpretation of Vatican II teaching. The bishops emphasise Holy Communion as the sacrament of existing unity and deny that there yet exists enough agreement in faith, both generally and specifically in regard to Holy Communion itself, for 'intercommunion'. They also do not accept that Anglican or Free Church Eucharists are fully 'valid'.

107

The Eucharist, Sacrament of Unity (2001) is the Church of England bishops' response to *One Bread, One Body*. The Anglicans assert that the fundamental unity given in baptism justifies the interim sharing of Holy Communion as an integral aid to the process of growing into communion. 'We do not believe that ... eucharistic communion must be reserved for full ecclesial communion, visibly and structurally expressed'. Though there are other points on which they dissent from the teaching of *One Bread, One Body* on eucharistic hospitality, this is the key one – that Holy Communion is a means towards the unity of the Church, not just a sign of unity existing or already achieved. Methodists would generally endorse this line.

108

Many Methodists now recognise that there is an immense amount to be learned from other Christian traditions. Increasingly, this is not just from those traditions which have long been established in Britain, but also from the World Church. The universal tradition and the local tradition need to be in constant dialogue, so that by sharing with our sisters and brothers each other's insights and practices, we may

all grow towards a fuller appreciation and expression of the complex mystery of Holy Communion.

Discussion question: What experience do you have of Holy Communion as celebrated in other traditions (denominations)?

Do you, or others in your church have helpful insights to share from experiences of Holy Communion in the context of other world cultures?

(x) Ecumenically sensitive issues

109
Once Christians from particular eucharistic communities begin to live alongside others their current practices will either be called into question or require justification. The issue of lay presidency is discussed in paragraphs 163 to 166 of the report *An Anglican Methodist Covenant* (2001), which includes the comment that the difference of polity on this issue between us and the Church of England 'can cause tension within LEPs'. When Methodists are involved with other Free Churches an opposite tension can arise where other Free Churches permit greater use of lay presidency than Methodism. Other issues such as the arrangements for the disposal of unused bread and wine, the use of non-alcoholic wine and the use of individual cups tend not to cause difficulty in relations with other Free Churches but are sensitive in LEPs involving Anglicans. We would hope to grow in positive appreciation of the best in every tradition.

110 **Presidency**
Methodism does have very definite rules about presidency at Holy Communion – both as to who may preside (paragraphs 126-132 below outline the ways in which successive Conferences have addressed this issue) and also as to what they are expected to do and say (for example, in the 'Guidelines for ordering a service of Holy Communion' contained in the *Methodist Worship Book)*. The Presiding minister must be an ordained presbyter or other person specifically authorised by the Conference. In some other traditions, the Presiding minister must be an episcopally ordained presbyter, and no exceptions are permitted. By contrast, some other traditions insist that anyone authorised by the *local* church community should be able to preside, and this may well include lay people. Methodists are usually happy to accept the eucharistic discipline of other Churches, and try not to act in any way that might cause offence. In LEPs, circumstances relating to presidency vary from case to case as negotiated. Methodists have different views as to whether it is ever appropriate for a Methodist who is not an

ordained presbyter to preside at Holy Communion of some other Free Church tradition. This whole question is linked to issues of ecclesiology and differing ways of understanding the relationship between the local church and Universal Church.

111 **Whose Communion is it?**

Methodists emphasise that Communion is the Communion of Christ, and of the whole Church. Holy Communion may be celebrated according to differing, denominationally authorised rites, but there is no such thing as a 'Methodist', 'Anglican' or other denominational Communion as such: there is only the one Holy Communion of the Universal Church, celebrated as the 'foretaste of the heavenly banquet'. Since all are called to this banquet, it is appropriate that as many as are already willing share in its foretaste now.

112 **Baptism and Confirmation**

Some traditions regard baptism as an absolute pre-requisite for receiving Holy Communion – describing Communion in such terms as 'the family meal of the Church'. Others would want to exclude no one, believing that Christ's hospitality is for all; nevertheless, they would expect anyone who wanted to become a regular communicant to avail themselves of the other great sacrament. Both these views are found among Methodists, and the stipulation of the 2000 Conference that those admitted to Communion should normally be baptised was much debated and is still controversial. In a similar way, there are varied views and practices amongst Christian traditions in regard to the relationship between confirmation (where practised) and first Communion.

113 **Admission to Communion**

In the spectrum of Christian thought, there has been a tension between those traditions and individuals who have emphasised Holy Communion as the Church's act, for which the Church has full authority to set regulations, including those of admission or exclusion, and those who have emphasised it as the Supper of the Lord from which the Church has no right to exclude any who come in faith seeking to meet the One who is the invisible host at his own Table. Our Lord's openness to sinners and his table fellowship with them, would seem to imply that none should be excluded from Holy Communion. This accords with Methodism's Arminianism. (See also paragraphs 133 to 135, which consider issues to do with baptism and the admission of children.)

114

There is perhaps an irresolvable tension here that explains why the Christian world has been so divided on the matter. Roman Catholics and Orthodox insist there must

be full agreement in faith and common acceptance of Church authority before there can be full eucharistic hospitality. Holy Communion must be a sign of already existing unity. The issue of eucharistic hospitality is linked to the question of how much unity in faith is required, the main 'reformation Churches', including Anglicans, being less exacting in this respect than the Roman Catholics and Orthodox. (For the Roman Catholic bishops of Britain and Ireland in their report, *One Bread, One Body* (1998), eucharistic hospitality is not a serious option. For the Church of England bishops, in their reply *The Eucharist: Sacrament of Unity* (2001), our common Christian Baptism justifies the interim sharing of Holy Communion.) Others believe the Table must be open. It is Christ and not the Church that is host. Commitment to him is all that is needed rather than doctrinal agreement or membership of a particular Church Communion. Holy Communion is the meal of the Pilgrim People of God, who are still on a journey towards the final promised fullness of fellowship in Church life (cf. Ephesians 5:27). As a means of grace, it builds up the body and leads it towards fuller unity. Therefore, it can and has been argued that participation in it is a means towards greater unity as well as acting as a sign of the existing, though not yet perfect, degree of unity. In recent years, the Church of England has shifted some way from the first position towards the second, though without going the whole way.

115
By virtue of our policy of an open Table, the Methodist Church does not exclude those of other traditions, but is sensitive towards those of other Churches whose discipline does not permit their communicants to receive elsewhere. When Methodists are in dialogue with the Roman Catholic and Orthodox traditions there will be a diversity of opinions as to whether mutual eucharistic hospitality is a means to the desired end of organic union or the final goal and consummation of the search. By conviction Methodists would claim that eucharistic sharing deepens the bonds between Christians and does not have to wait for the formal and final stages of visible unity. In the responses to the Lima Report '*Baptism, Eucharist and Ministry*' British Methodists found no outstanding issue more important to them than the principle of the Lord's Supper as a 'converting ordinance' to which they held by conviction and the 'open table' which they now perceive as 'fundamental to their own eucharistic faith and practice'.

116 **Alcoholic wine/unleavened bread**
Some argue that the elements must be the same as those used by Christ in the Upper Room. Others argue that it is appropriate to use ordinary, leavened bread and non-alcoholic wine. In some LEPs, there are compromises, and alcoholic and non-alcoholic wine may both be available at the same Eucharist.

117 **Disposal of the elements**

This is a particularly difficult issue, since views as to what constitutes 'reverent disposal' vary. Some traditions insist the only reverent way is consumption at the end of the service; others feel throwing the elements away, even 'sharing them with the birds as another part of God's creation' is acceptable. Many, in other traditions, are horrified by this practice and Methodists will want to think very carefully about the need not to scandalise others unnecessarily. Consumption at the end of the service is the most widely recognised form of reverent disposal across the Christian Churches. It does not **of itself** commit one to any particular view of the status of the remaining elements.

118 **The Common Cup**

The main reason for advocating the 'common cup' is theological: it testifies far more eloquently to *koinonia* than separate glasses or cups. However, a matter of great concern to many people in the use of a 'common cup' or chalice is the likelihood of the spread of infection. Expert opinion is that this need not be a serious problem – the risk is remote, and there is no evidence to suggest that there have been problems in those Churches that have centuries of tradition of using a common cup. Infectious agents such as viruses survive only a matter of a second or two on a silver chalice, and this risk can be reduced by wiping the rim after each communicant. There may be a greater risk with other sorts of chalices, e.g. pottery, due to the uneven surface, which may harbour micro-organisms. It makes very little difference whether alcoholic or non-alcoholic wine is used. *Koinonia* is about risk of all sorts and there is no reason to be deterred from using the common cup by a level of danger that is no greater than that involved in breathing in each other's germs at any service. Individual glasses were introduced (around the start of the twentieth century) into Free Churches as much to facilitate the custom of distribution to communicants as they sat in the pews as for any reasons of hygiene, and not specifically in the context of the use of non-alcoholic Communion wine.

119 **Frequency of Communion services**

This is also a live issue within ecumenical partnerships. Where only the Free Churches are involved the matter is not nearly so difficult to resolve as when the Church of England is within the partnership. Where there has been a weekly tradition of early Communions and parish Eucharists the 'stronger' tradition is likely to prevail.

Discussion question: How important are the issues discussed in this section to you? Is it vital to maintain the 'traditional' Methodist position on them? If not, where would you be prepared to compromise?

F PREVIOUS CONFERENCE STATEMENTS AND DECISIONS RELATING TO HOLY COMMUNION

120
Methodist theology and practice of the Lord's Supper rests on the Methodist Church's foundation document, the Deed of Union (1932). Clause 4 ('Doctrine') includes the words, "The Methodist Church recognises two sacraments, namely Baptism and the Lord's Supper as of divine appointment and of perpetual obligation of which it is the privilege and duty of members of the Methodist Church to avail themselves." Clause 9 ('Privileges and Duties of Membership') states, 'It is the privilege and duty of members of the Methodist Church to avail themselves of the two sacraments, namely Baptism and the Lord's Supper.' New members are to be received during an act of worship including the sacrament of the Lord's Supper (Clause 8b) and persistent absence from the Lord's Supper is one of the grounds for instigating the process that can result in cessation of membership (Clause 10a).

121
Aspects of the Methodist Church's present practice are embodied in Standing Orders 011 (which deals with the procedures for authorisation by the Conference of named lay persons to preside in cases of deprivation) and 609 (which deals with the practice of 'Extended Communion,' whereby elements set aside at a previous celebration of Holy Communion are received during acts of worship in homes – including nursing and retirement homes -, hospitals and hospices). Question 49 of *A Catechism for the use of the people called Methodists* describes the Lord's Supper in terms of Christ's presence with his worshipping people, receiving him by faith and with thanksgiving as they eat the bread and drink the wine: the service is an act of thanksgiving, recollection, proclamation, unity, sacrifice and a foretaste of the heavenly banquet.

122
What is distinctive about the Methodist Church in respect of Holy Communion and what it shares with other World Churches have been set forth in considered Conference responses to various major ecumenical statements namely, Edinburgh (1937), Lund (1952), Lima (1982) and the Roman Catholic encyclical *Ut Unum Sint* (1995). These responses suggest that what is shared with other Churches is first, that the Lord's Supper (Eucharist) is 'of divine appointment and perpetual obligation'. Second, that it stands as a memorial of Christ's life, death and resurrection. Third, that it is a sacrament of his 'real presence' and sacrificial self-giving. Fourth, that it is an

eschatological anticipation of fellowship with him in his eternal kingdom. However, it is also made clear that there are issues that deeply distinguish Methodist understanding and practice from those of some other Churches, such as questions of eucharistic presidency, frequency of celebration, and the nature of Christ's presence. These issues are the subjects of on-going study, debate and search for mutual understanding and reconciling principles.

123
A limited exposition of the Methodist Church as 'sacramental society' was developed in the 1937 Conference report *The Nature of the Christian Church*. This emphasises the continuity of the Methodist Church and its legitimate place in the Holy Catholic Church – the Church Universal. It also holds that the Methodist Church (following its founder John Wesley) lays great stress on sacramental worship and recognises two divinely appointed sacraments – Baptism and The Lord's Supper.

124
The 1999 Conference statement *Called To Love and Praise* was the first attempt by the Conference since the 1937 Report to explore systematically Methodist understanding of itself as Church. Not a great deal is said in this report about the Sacrament of the Lord's Supper but it clearly sees Holy Communion as central to the life and worship of the Methodist Church and strongly maintains that "in this typical act of worship Holy Communion strengthens and, in a sense, makes the Church." In this the partnership of ordained ministers and lay people remains vital to the work and well-being of the Church, though it is thought appropriate that the Lord's Supper should mainly be celebrated under the authority of those who are representative of the whole Church.

125
In between those reports the Conference has received and considered many Memorials from Circuits and Districts and Notices of Motion from individuals and groups concerning beliefs and practices surrounding the administration of the Lord's Supper. This is evidence both of the growth of interest in the centrality of this service in Methodist worship and at the same time it reveals the diversity of belief about what is authentically Methodist about our doctrine and practice. In response to this stream of Memorials and Notices of Motion the Conference has, over the years, commissioned and subsequently received or adopted no less than twenty reports and responses having a bearing on this important topic. Of these, sixteen have dealt with questions regarding presidency at the Lord's Supper.

126
The 1946 Report *Lay Administration of the Sacraments* began with these affirmations:

- There are two divinely appointed sacraments – Baptism and the Lord's Supper. Provision for their orderly and regular celebration must therefore be made.
- The *general usage* (in the Methodist Church) is that ministers should *normally* preside.
- The principle of *duly authorised* lay administration is upheld.

127
These affirmations, now embodied in Standing Orders 011 and 609, represent something of a compromise between the different views and practices prevailing among the three Connexions that were party to the 1932 *Deed of Union*. Over the years these affirmations have been maintained although in successive Conference replies and reports there has been a tendency for the second to be stressed at the expense of the third. The criterion for allowing persons other than ministers to preside has been 'deprivation'. In a situation of decline in the number of ministers combined with a desire for more frequent celebration of Holy Communion, what constitutes a situation of deprivation has been a matter of contention and the subject of some of the Memorials mentioned above.

128
More recent statements of the Conference have attempted to give the term 'deprivation' more precise definition. Guidelines on how it is to be measured are now incorporated into CPD (*The Constitutional Practice and Discipline of the Methodist Church*).

129
The primary focus, then, of the on-going debate has been not the importance and significance of Holy Communion, which is widely though not universally endorsed, but the question of who can preside at the Service of the Lord's Supper. The debate has been between those who, on the one hand, believe that presidency is the sole prerogative of ordained ministers (with concessions under strictly limited circumstances marked by 'local deprivation' and/or a 'missionary situation') and those who believe that more widespread provision should be made for suitably qualified lay people to be authorised, subject to the principles of orderliness and supervision. However, the principle laid down in the Deed of Union of 1932 that regulations about presidency at the Lord's Supper are matters of Church order rather than fundamental doctrine has never been abrogated.

130
A report of 1984 commended the practice of *Extending Communion*. One of the arguments put forward for an extension or relaxation of the rules for lay authorisation concerns the needs of people unable to attend normal church services because of sickness or infirmity. Extended Communion is when a layperson authorised by the Church Council takes the bread and wine from a public celebration presided over by a minister to those who are sick or housebound. The Conference has authorised an appropriate form of service, emphasising that Extended Communion is not a service of Holy Communion as such, but an extension of the celebration of the local church, in which bread and wine set aside at an earlier service of Holy Communion are shared.

131
Two reports (*Ordination* 1974 and *The Methodist Diaconal Order* 1995) have addressed the question of the role of deacons, probationer ministers and ministers in local appointments in relation to presidency at the Lord's Supper. Guidance was provided in these reports restating the case that ministers (presbyters) in full connexion have a unique duty to preside by virtue of their ordination, that presidency is not normally part of the functions of a deacon and that the circumstances in which they and probationer ministers in both connexional and local appointments should be given 'special dispensations' to preside should be the same as for 'lay' people in the Church.

132
The 1996 report *Authorisation to Preside at the Lord's Supper* attempted to draw together and reiterate principles set out in various previous reports. It addressed specific proposals and arguments for widening and normalising the use of lay presidency. In particular, it rejected the argument that the doctrine of 'the priesthood of all believers' necessarily implies that any person can preside at the Lord's Supper. It restated the principle that presidency is an essential part of what a minister is and that it is a 'duty', not a 'right'. It rejected the idea of any necessary connection between being in pastoral charge of a congregation and presidency. Presidency of ministers is based on Church Order (or Structure) not on a local relationship. Finally, it brought out the ecumenical dimensions that point away from a need for radical change at the moment. The final recommendation was for no change to the principle of lay authorisation only in circumstances of deprivation but that the understanding of deprivation 'be widened', to include the needs and opportunities for home and hospital Communion, as well as in churches.

133
Two further major reports (*Children and Holy Communion* 1987 and 2000) have addressed the issue of the participation in the Lord's Supper of persons other than those with full, adult membership status. This includes what has been called eucharistic hospitality – the practice of inviting people who are practising members of other Churches – but the main focus has been on whether children, whether baptised or not and at what age, should be invited to full participation. The precise meaning and implication of the (now) traditional Methodist invitation to 'all who love the Lord Jesus Christ' was explored. The 1987 Report noted that pressure for change in the Church has come from a growing awareness and appreciation of the Lord's Supper and a growing understanding of the faith development of children. Parents and children have begun to ask why they (the children) should be excluded. Guidelines were proposed based on the theological principle that baptism is the only qualification for entry into the family of the Church and that children have a rightful place alongside parents and other adults at the Lord's Table. However it was stressed that great sensitivity to the faith aspirations and potentialities of children was needed but that "the time has come to move forward and encourage children to participate fully in the Lord's Supper". A set of 'guidelines' was proposed as an interim measure.

134
After some years of implementation of these guidelines, further study and consultation the Conference in 2000 accepted its most recent report entitled *Children and Holy Communion*. The report was based, in part, on a careful survey that gathered evidence of current practice and attitudes about the participation of children in services of Holy Communion across the whole Connexion. The report recommended that it be considered normal practice for baptised children, as members of the Body of Christ, to participate in Holy Communion by receiving bread and wine, irrespective of age.

135
The 'guidelines' set out in 1987 were replaced by a policy statement (now in a process of 'reception') that encompasses and is binding upon the Methodist Church as a whole. This covers such matters as what is normal practice regarding children and Holy Communion; encouragement toward baptism for participating adults and children not already baptised; opportunities for learning about the sacraments to be considered an integral part of Church life; consultation with and consent of parents; sensitivity to the beliefs of denominational partners in ecumenical partnerships; and sharing in the whole service by children.

136

In conclusion, we may say that in the successive documents coming from the Conference since 1932 there has been a gradual development of our thinking and practice with regard to the Lord's Supper. There have been some adjustments to the position implied by the Deed of Union, sometimes accompanied by subtle changes of language and expression, which have had the effect of shifting emphases and interpretations in significant ways. These adjustments point to the way in which Holy Communion has come to play a more significant role in the life of Methodist congregational life. At the same time, diverse views and varying practices continue to be found across the Connexion.

Discussion questions: Are you comfortable with the conclusions that the Conference has reached on these issues (e.g. on the admission of children to Holy Communion)? How can we do justice to the diversity of opinions within the Methodist Church? What are the tolerable limits to diversity? Where is there need for further development of the Methodist Church's thinking?

G THEOLOGICAL RESOURCES

In this section, we supplement the largely descriptive material in the earlier sections with some more general resource material that informs and is informed by Methodist belief and practice as we have described it.

(i) Language and the Sacraments

137
Religious language, particularly language about the sacraments, is not the language of everyday conversation: words are used in different ways, although the subtleties of this are not always appreciated. The difference can also lead to misunderstanding and confusion. Fortunately, present-day understandings of language and its relationship to reality have positive implications for talking about sacraments.

138
Three things need to be said about the language used by the Church in the ritual re-enactment of the sacrament of the Lord's Supper. The first is that the language used is far from arbitrary. It has a unique history of use. The language used reflects or is derived from not only biblical origins but also from the accumulated liturgical resources of the worshipping Church over its 2000 years of history. When we perform the actions and say the words of the Holy Communion we express and affirm the continuity of our faith with Christians from the earliest times and with the 'saints' throughout the ages. We also implicitly identify ourselves with the worldwide Church seeking communion with its Lord in similar terms.

139
The second feature of the language used in the service is that it draws inevitably on the riches of pictorial, figurative and metaphorical forms to reach through and beyond the literal and the prosaic to that which is ultimately beyond human language to express – to the mystery of God. Christian preachers, poets, theologians and worship leaders have always striven to express the inexpressible and draw listener and speaker alike into an experience of the divine. To do so they have had to stretch language to its limits using simile, analogy, and metaphor.

140
The word 'sacrament' derives from a Latin word usually used to translate the New Testament Greek word *mysterion*, meaning 'mystery'. A sacrament has been familiarly

described as 'an outward and visible sign of an inward and spiritual grace'. A sign is an indicator, a pointer, but the language of the sacrament of the Lord's Supper indicates that it is more than that. It is a symbol and symbols, in human experience, do more than merely point or indicate. A symbol can be said to be an object, event, action or person that establishes a connection – a bridge between two worlds. The world of everyday sense experience and relationships and the world of meaning, significance and value, a world of the spirit. A bridge is a crossing point, a means of communication, and a place where two realms meet. Another way of thinking about symbols is as illumination. The symbolic nature of the language of Holy Communion makes it a powerful instrument to extend our vision, stimulate the imagination and deepen understanding by exposing to us a realm of experience that would otherwise be inaccessible.

141
Some contemporary theologians make much of what they call the 'sacramental principle' in their discussion of the total context of the sacraments. The Roman Catholic theologian Edward Schillebeeckx talks of Christ as 'the sacrament of God's presence' and of Christ as the 'primal sacrament', indicating that Christ communicated God's love and presence through his deeds and actions in their total embodiment as well as through his words and teaching. Such an emphasis corresponds with the fullness of human communication in which sign and gesture play a role, sometimes complementary to words, sometimes adding a force or dimension that cannot come from words alone.

142
Unfortunately, when figures of speech become common currency through endless repetition their function as symbols can be forgotten. The natural tendency then is for them to die as images and be taken merely as literal descriptions to be accepted or rejected as such. This is true not only of religious language but also in science where 'metaphors' become elaborated into 'models' and serve, temporarily at least, to confine the mind to seeing things in only one particular way. The language of the service of Holy Communion is shot through with metaphor and figurative expressions which can come to appear to be literal descriptions of things as they really are and even the only way they can be described. This is a mistake. For example:

'... *light* of our salvation'
'... *breathed into life* the desire of your heart ...'
'... with *the full chorus* of your creation ...'
'*Pour out* your spirit ...'
'... the grace of God *has dawned* upon the world ...'
'...You did not leave us *in darkness* ...'

The language we use in the Sacrament of the Lord's Supper does indeed refer to historical events and plain everyday objects such as bread and wine, mundane activities like eating and drinking, but at the same time uses them as symbols. It thereby has the mysterious capacity of evoking in us an awareness and an experience of a different, more significant reality.

143
There is also the danger that we invest too heavily in particular forms of words – as if the words themselves have some inherent or even magical quality irrespective of who says them and in what context: that unless this particular form of words is used nothing happens and nothing can happen. In this view, meticulous adherence to a form, no matter what, automatically brings about what is asserted. It can be thought that even slight deviations from the precise form vitiate their effectiveness. But this is to reduce the language of the service to a kind of formula.

144
A third feature of language relevant to our understanding of Holy Communion is what saying the words commits us to. Christians are used to the notion of the Word of God as denoting not just speech but the effective activity of God in the world. *Our* words too are used to act upon our world, to change things, to bring things about, to enact things. This is most clearly seen when we make a promise. The act of uttering the words 'I promise' commits me to a course of action. Unless they are overtly spoken (or written) no change in the situation takes place. But not only promises enact things. Many of our utterances can be thought of as 'speech acts'. In the speaking of the words, 'I take you to be my wife/husband' in a wedding ceremony, the declaration actually establishes the new relationship in law. The words of a declaring officer at an election actually inaugurate the successful candidate as the elected Member of Parliament for that particular constituency. There are also cases where words and actions are linked such as in the naming of a ship by breaking a bottle against its hull and the opening of a road or building by cutting a ribbon. Many of our utterances and actions can be said to have this same property. In the service of Holy Communion we are doing things with words and actions – acknowledging, praising, confessing, committing, promising, identifying, binding. If this is so, then in the language we use and the actions we perform we become deeply involved. We have to be sure that the words we use reflect and are in accordance with authentic Christian experience and discipleship, the historic faith of the Church, with our own doctrinal standards and with scripture.

145
A service of Holy Communion has been likened to the performance of a great musical work – a symphony or sonata. Any particular performance is a creative re-enactment of the original but the uniqueness of the original creative act by which the work was first conceived by the composer is not called into question. There is an organic and intrinsic connection between the original creation and the current performance. The performance does not repeat the original creative act but makes the result actual and live as a present (and perhaps, thrilling) experience. Performers and listeners alike in some sense become participants in what the composer has created. The heart of the service of Holy Communion is an action or series of actions – the blessing, giving and taking of bread and wine in a manner determined by our Lord. These physical actions symbolise both the occasion and the continuing process by which divine grace impinges on human lives and mysteriously enters them. The actions are given context, meaning and significance by symbolic words, spoken and heard before during and after their performance. In the Lord's Supper, the original act of saving grace remains unique and unrepeatable but the language of the service recreates in words the original drama and allows the worshipper to become both participant and beneficiary in the saving act.

146
Holy Communion is far more than a visual aid to the Word (though preaching properly forms part of its totality in celebration). It takes account of our total 'embodiedness' as it involves word, gesture, action, taste, all visible actions. In particular it is action. It is not just words, not even just words that do something to bread and wine and us, but gesture, breaking (hence the importance of the fraction in Holy Communion), taking and eating that are dynamic. It is highly significant that it was in the breaking of bread that the disciples at Emmaus recognised the Lord (Luke 24:35).

(ii) Nine key themes in the theology of Holy Communion, drawn from the Bible and Christian Tradition

147
This section presents the biblical background which informs Methodist understandings of each of these themes, indicates the degree or absence of emphasis placed on each, and how these interpretations feature in conversations with our ecumenical partners. As this is largely a descriptive exercise, no attempt is made here to discuss the differing levels of authority between, say, different biblical

passages and later ecclesiastical tradition. These matters are in any case much debated and space does not permit justice to be done to all the issues involved. Nor do we enter into debate about the significance of the silence about any sharing of bread and wine during Jesus's final meal with his disciples as recounted in the Gospel of John. What is offered here, in brief, is a series of insights distilled from Methodist thinking, to complement the findings of the survey about the value of Holy Communion to Methodists. It is our hope that this may provide a foundation for basic learning about its meaning.

Thanksgiving (Eucharist) – *"He gave thanks"*

148

The emphasis on Holy Communion as the Church's great act of thanksgiving, inseparably linked to Christ's offering of thanks to the Father, is both ancient and contemporary. The 1982 Lima Report *Baptism Eucharist and Ministry* cites thanksgiving to the Father as the first of the great themes of this service. It was typically Jewish of Jesus to 'give thanks' to God the Father over food. We see this in the feeding of the five thousand, where the synoptic writers use the verb 'to bless' (Greek: *eulogein*; Matthew 14:19, Mark 6:41 and Luke 9:16a). The Gospel of John uses (John 6:11) the verb 'to give thanks' (*eucharistein*), which is also used in the narrative of the feeding of the four thousand in Matthew 15:36 and Mark 8:6. The latter verb is used of Paul when saying grace (Acts 27:35). The verb *eucharistein* is also used for the words of Jesus over the bread and cup at the institution of the Lord's Supper in the Synoptic Gospels and by St Paul in 1 Corinthians 11. The one exception is the use of the verb *eulogein* by Mark when Jesus gives thanks over the bread. Thanksgiving in the Jewish tradition always has a purpose. (In Leviticus 7:11-18 a sacrifice is offered for thanksgiving. In Deuteronomy 12:7 there is a connection made between eating and rejoicing and in Psalm 116:10-11 the psalmist repays the Lord for all his goodness by lifting up the cup of salvation.) In the Gospel of John, immediately before Jesus performs the greatest of his signs, the raising of Lazarus, he raises his eyes to heaven and offers 'thanksgiving' to the Father (John 11:41). In the Biblical tradition the custom is to give thanks to God the Father for what he has done or is about to do: to remember all the benefits of divine Providence. At the Last Supper Jesus gave thanks ('made eucharist') over the bread and cup for God's goodness and saving work. The other side of the cross and the resurrection the Church 'gives thanks' for a saving work that now includes the whole Christ event.

149
Early Christian documents contain instructions as to how to 'give thanks'. They widen the scope from thanksgiving for the sacrificial death of Christ to thanksgiving for the knowledge and scope of salvation and for the good things of creation. The tradition of giving thanks for the total scope of God's work was to a large extent lost in the Western medieval tradition where the emphasis was upon thanksgiving for the death of Christ rather than celebration of his resurrection. The Liturgical Movement of the nineteenth and twentieth centuries helped restore an emphasis on the Eucharist as an act of thanksgiving for the total scope of creation and redemption. This broader understanding had remained strong in the Eastern Christian tradition and was re-emphasised also in the Roman Catholic tradition from the 1960s.

150
The Wesleys emphasised the celebratory nature of Holy Communion in some of their most lyrical hymns. The emphasis from the death of the Wesleys till the early years of the twentieth century was more on the solemn memorial of Christ's death, thankfully observed but in a sober rather than in a celebratory style, an ethos sustained both by the traditional 1662 Anglican liturgy and by the shorter rites in the non-Wesleyan traditions. The celebratory aspect of the Holy Communion as thanksgiving to the Father for all the great acts of redemption was recovered in the 1975 *Methodist Service Book*. It is even more vividly and variably expressed in the various seasonal 'Great Prayers of Thanksgiving' within the present *Methodist Worship Book*.

151
The 1985 response of British Methodism to the Lima Report stressed that there were some Methodists who resisted the idea of seeing the Lord's Supper as primarily 'Eucharist' or thanksgiving and preferred to stress it as solemn memorial of the Lord's death and solemn personal communion with Him. Such views still prevail in some quarters, not just in Methodism, but also in other Free Churches and some Churches in the Reformed tradition. On the other hand, it is true that the trend in the Anglican, Roman Catholic, Lutheran and Methodist traditions, as manifested in liturgical revision, has been increasingly to stress the concept of thanksgiving for the totality of God's work. One can perhaps now speak of a consensus in these traditions, and perhaps among many 'Reformed' on this aspect of Holy Communion.

Life in Unity (Koinonia) – *"We are one body"*

152
Both Jesus and Paul regarded the sharing at meals as means of breaking down barriers

and building up relationships. Jesus ate and drank with sinners (Mark 2:15f., Matthew 9:9f.). In a famous reference to the Lord's Supper Paul spoke of the bread and cup as a means of having communion or participation in the body and blood of Christ (1 Corinthians 10:16b-17). Conversely, greedy or inconsiderate behaviour at the Lord's Supper could break the Church's fellowship and unity symbolised among other things by the one loaf and the common cup (1 Corinthians 11:17-34). The meal of divine love (the *agape*) and the Lord's Supper were not necessarily distinct and hence the quality of the relationships of participants to each other was paramount. In John 13:18 the quoting of Psalm 41:9 'the one who ate my bread has lifted his heel against me' is making reference to the intimacy of sharing table fellowship with Christ. The action of Judas breaks the *koinonia*. The event of eating and drinking together is both a sign and a means of being in community. The parable of the prodigal son ends with an invitation to a meal of joy and reconciliation (Luke 15:23-24, 32). The post-resurrection communion of Christ with his disciples is most frequently presented in overt or explicit eucharistic meals (e.g. Luke 24:13-35, 41-43, John 21:4-14 and Acts 10:41). In the great fourfold summary of the life of the Church in Acts 2:42 the disciples are united in the apostles' teaching, in fellowship, in the breaking of bread and in the prayers. More generally, fellowship with Christ was at the heart of Paul's gospel. For Paul the believer shared in Christ's humility, suffering and glory. In the First Letter of John believers share in the communion that exists between the Father and the Son.

153

This understanding of Holy Communion as creating, sustaining and expressing intimate community in the Body of Christ continued to be strong in the early Church up to the time of Augustine. But this emphasis was later largely lost when much of Europe became nominally Christian. A sense of Holy Communion as an awesome rite carried out by the clergy on behalf of the people prevailed over the earlier concept of corporate celebration. As a result, many became afraid to receive Communion frequently because they felt 'unworthy'. The act of Communion was increasingly seen as an act of personal devotion for those who were particularly committed rather than as an act of solidarity in the Body of Christ. Such attitudes survived the Reformation, despite the wishes of the Reformers. In recent years, the pattern has changed in most Western Churches so that few regular members and adherents fail to receive Communion when it is celebrated.

154

In Methodism, many factors, such as infrequency of celebration and the tendency to 'tack' the Lord's Supper on to the end of an 'ordinary' service, led to many habitually neglecting Communion despite repeated Conference statements. However, the

Methodist practice of receiving and dismissing 'tables' of communicants may have helped to preserve a sense of the corporate dimension in Holy Communion. This sense can be seen in the line 'never without His people seen' in *Hymns & Psalms* 622. Several services of Holy Communion in the *Methodist Worship Book* include the words, 'though we are many, we are one body, because we all share in one bread'.

155
Ecumenically, there is wide agreement that Holy Communion demonstrates the oneness of Christ and his people. 'It is in the Eucharist that the community of God's people is most fully manifested' (*Baptism, Eucharist and Ministry* para M19). The Lima Report *Baptism, Eucharist and Ministry* brought this idea of *koinonia* or community to the fore. The unity and communion of the whole Church and of each member of it, one with another, and of all with the Father through the Son in the Spirit is at the heart of Holy Communion. Therefore Holy Communion both creates and expresses the one communion and fellowship of all Christians. Those in more 'Catholic' traditions would particularly emphasise this, while some in more 'Protestant' traditions might demur from the phrase 'most fully'. They would grant that Holy Communion certainly does manifest the unity of believers, but would want to add that unity can also be demonstrated in other acts of worship and common life. For some the emphasis would be on the unity of the believers in an individual congregation; others would emphasise unity with the Universal Church across time and space.

156
There is continuing division over whether eucharistic sharing is a means towards greater unity, and in that context appropriate for Christians in Churches that are still formally separated, or whether, as Roman Catholics and Orthodox continue to believe and practise, it is normally only appropriate for those who are already united in faith and Church life (see paragraphs 113-115 for a fuller discussion). Until the early twentieth century the latter was also the normal view of Methodism and some other Churches in the Reformation tradition. In Methodism, the class ticket or some other device was a ticket of admission to Communion. For some, open eucharistic hospitality is inherent in the sacrament as a memorial of Christ's openness to sinners demonstrated in the table fellowship of his lifetime. In recent years, Methodism has practised generous eucharistic hospitality for believers of all Christian traditions.

Remembering (Anamnesis) – "Do this in remembrance of me"

157
The word '*anamnesis*' is derived from 1 Corinthians 11:24 and belongs to the Lukan-

Pauline versions of the institution of the Lord's Supper. No one English word expresses the combined meanings in *anamnesis* of calling into present reality a fresh outpouring of the saving power of the event remembered. This is the point at which the underlying theologies of the Passover and of Holy Communion are in parallel. An Exodus or supreme act of divine delivery is at hand on the first occasion of both Jewish ritual meals – Jewish Passover and Last Supper. The gift present in the original saving event is appropriated in the subsequent repetitions of both ritual meals. *Anamnesis* is about renewed contact with the original source of blessing – the God who saves through the Exodus in the Passover and who saves through the death and resurrection of Christ in Holy Communion. The few early eucharistic texts that survive from the post-New Testament period recite the events of Jesus' saving death much as the Passover liturgy, of a similar period, recited the events of the Exodus.

158
The understanding of Christ's words, 'Do this in remembrance of me' has varied widely throughout Christian history. Some have taken them to imply a 'bare memorial', i.e. a simple act of thankful remembrance of Christ's sacrifice. Others have seen them as involving a very vivid 'calling to mind' and 'making present' sacramentally of Christ's victory. The question has been bedevilled, since the Reformation, by fears that Holy Communion might somehow be seen either as a repetition of or addition to Christ's unique sacrifice. The Reformers also wished to combat any idea that Holy Communion could in any way be seen as a meritorious work that it was necessary to perform in order to achieve salvation.

159
In recent years a renewed interest in Biblical understandings of '*anamnesis*' has helped to bring about a high degree of convergence between the main Christian traditions. However, as the 'Lima' responses show, this convergence is by no means fully accepted at the official level in all Churches, nor has it necessarily been 'received' by all the faithful. The current understanding is that '*anamnesis*' is a highly dynamic concept which involves bringing into the present the continued fruitfulness and efficacy of Christ's saving work. Our sister United Methodist Church puts it thus:

> 'In terms of the congregation's appropriation of the reality of Christ's presence, the *anamnesis* (memorial, remembrance, representation) means that past, present and future coincide in the sacramental event. All that Jesus Christ means in his person and redemption is brought forth from history to our present experience that is also a foretaste of the future fulfilment of God's unobstructed

reign. And this presence is made a reality for us by the working of God's Spirit, whom we call down by invocation (*epiclesis*), both upon the gifts and upon the people'. (*Churches Respond to Baptism, Eucharist and Ministry*, vol. 2, p188 World Council of Churches 1986)

160
The Wesleys had a dynamic sense of 'memorial', as can be evidenced from such a hymn as 'Victim divine, Thy grace we claim' (*HP* 629) with such lines as:

> Thou standest now before the throne

and, in particular, the concluding verse:

> We need not now go up to heaven
> To bring the long sought Saviour down;
> Thou art to all already given,
> Thou dost ev'n now thy banquet crown:
> To every faithful soul appear,
> And show thy real presence here!

161
Later Methodism, however, largely lost this dynamic sense of the memorial. Nineteenth century Communion services were largely seen as solemn acts of remembrance rather than as joyful celebrations of past victory and future glory being made dynamically present and available. From the mid-twentieth century, Methodist involvement in the Liturgical and Ecumenical Movements has meant an increasing appropriation of the renewed dynamic understanding of the memorial, strongly reflected in the liturgical revisions of 1975 and 1999. For some in Methodism, however, the former emphasis remains.

Sacrifice – *"... For you"*

162
In Romans 12:1 the members of the Church are asked by Paul to present their bodies as a living sacrifice, and this is to be considered as their spiritual worship. The writer of the First Letter of Peter also speaks of the Christian community offering 'spiritual sacrifices'. The writer to the Hebrews (Hebrews 13:15) exhorts the Christian community 'through Christ' continually 'to offer up a sacrifice of praise to God, that is the fruit of lips that acknowledge his name.' In other words sincere worship offered through Christ is a sacrifice of praise.

163
It is perfectly reasonable to regard Holy Communion as one of the actions of the Christian community in which a sacrifice of praise is offered to the Father through the Son. Holy Communion is a sacrifice of praise because it is a means of offering praise to God through Christ.

164
The image of sacrifice is important to the New Testament. As well as the sacrifice of the Christian community, which is a sacrifice of praise offered through Christ, there is the image of the atoning sacrifice of Christ, the understanding of Jesus as High Priest and the picture of him as the Lamb of God who takes away the sin of the world. The community both offers the sacrifice of its own self in obedience, service and commitment – a living sacrifice – and proclaims the atoning sacrifice of Christ. The sacrifice of Christ is the one and only means whereby the Church's sacrifice of its praise and of itself can be offered. The New Testament Eucharist celebrates the inseparability of Christ's sacrifice and ours.

165
The New Testament is written out of the conviction that 'Jesus is Lord', but the fact that he died by crucifixion was a huge scandal which needed to be addressed. The first Christians drew upon their theological resources, the Scriptures and Jewish tradition, to find explanations for the death of Christ and for metaphors by which to understand it. In so doing they found the idea of 'sacrifice' to be a particularly helpful one. In their understanding, the sacrificial system, in all its complexity, was God's gift to them as a 'means of grace'. It provided ways of worship in which, in different types of sacrifice, praise and thanksgiving could be offered, dedication expressed and obedience learned and, in the sacrifices for sin, guilt assuaged and forgiveness received. What must be remembered is that the sacrifices for sin were not intended to persuade God to change his mind about sinners, but to be the way God himself had given for them to express their repentance and then to hear, primarily in the 'sprinkled blood', God's declaration of forgiveness to all who had repented in this way.

166
When we turn to the New Testament accounts of the Last Supper we read that Jesus explicitly tells the disciples that they must 'take' and 'drink' what is 'given' for them – his body and his blood. The association between the bread and wine and his self-offering or sacrifice is thus built into the story from the beginning. It is therefore easy to see how the understanding of Holy Communion as in some sense a sacrifice developed very early in Christian tradition. Some of the earliest eucharistic prayers

draw on Old Testament formulae concerning sacrifice, though always insisting on the uniqueness of the particular sacrifice Christ offered. The bringing together of this kind of language and the understanding that the worship which is offered is itself a sacrificial act led naturally, perhaps inevitably, to the notion of 'eucharistic sacrifice'. The *Didache* – a Christian text dating from the late first or second century – refers to sacrifice three times in its chapter on the Eucharist (Chapter 14). One reference is to making confession 'that our sacrifice may be pure'; another is to being reconciled with others 'that our sacrifice be not polluted'. The third reference alludes to Malachi 1:11, commenting, 'In every place and time offer me a pure sacrifice: for I am a great King, says the Lord.' There is a touch of ambiguity here. Is the sacrifice the act of offering worship or specifically the offering of bread and wine? In the Western Church (unlike the Eastern), Eucharistic sacrifice has always been a controversial idea.

167
Almost all Christians would be happy to accept the phrase 'sacrifice of praise and thanksgiving' (Hebrews 13:15) as applicable to Holy Communion. Most would probably also accept that it is a particularly appropriate occasion for rededication to Christ, and offering ourselves to Him as 'a living sacrifice'. For some Methodists the celebration of Holy Communion at the Covenant Service underlines this point. More controversial is the concept of Holy Communion as a sacrifice offered by the Church in union with the ascended and interceding Christ. All the Reformers had difficulty with this concept, since they feared that it detracted from the sole sufficiency of the 'full, perfect and sufficient sacrifice, satisfaction and oblation once offered' on Calvary, as expressed by Cranmer. They also feared it turned Holy Communion into a 'work' and undermined the doctrine of justification by grace through faith. Roman Catholics and Orthodox continue to insist on the sacrificial nature of Holy Communion, arguing that it makes 'sacramentally present' the paschal event and its fruits.

168
The Wesleys certainly held a doctrine of eucharistic sacrifice, as illustrated in Section 4 of their *Hymns on the Lord's Supper* and particularly in such a verse as (from no. 105 *'O God of our forefathers, hear'*):

> With solemn faith we offer up,
> And spread before Thy glorious eyes
> The only ground of all our hope,
> That precious bleeding sacrifice,
> Which brings Thy grace on sinners down,
> And perfects all our souls in one.

The Wesleys inherited notions of the eucharist as implying a sacrifice from Dean Brevint and other 17th century Anglican divines.

169
Nineteenth century Methodism was normally dismissive of such a concept of eucharistic sacrifice. More recently, Methodism has been hesitant on the subject. The first two reports of the international Roman Catholic-Methodist dialogue recorded Methodist fears about the language of sacrifice being used to imply that Christ was 'still being sacrificed', while recording that Methodists were happy to talk of 'pleading the sacrifice here and now' and to talk of 'the sacrifice of ourselves in union with the Christ who offered Himself to the Father'. These two offerings, Christ's and ours, are joined together in the one sacrifice of praise and thanksgiving. The latter coheres with recent Roman Catholic emphasis on the unity of the whole Christ, Head and members. Methodists would be willing to concede that the supreme occasion for the celebration of this conjoined sacrifice, Christ's and ours, is Holy Communion.

170
It can be argued that, in Methodism, the emphasis is primarily on the 'sacrifice of praise', as exemplified in such a hymn as *HP* 35, 'Glory, love and praise and honour' which was originally written as a eucharistic hymn. Albert Outler sums up much that we might say about memorial and sacramental availability:

> The Eucharist is the Christian memorial par excellence, because in it the historical preface and the new miracle of Christ's living presence are fused. But the Eucharist is also more than a memorial, for in his *full sacramental reality* Jesus Christ is really and truly present here and now. It is a sacrament in which an historical memory has been imbedded as an essential ingredient. (Outler, A. *The Christian Tradition and the Unity we Seek*, 1964)

171
Perhaps a statement from the Lutheran-Roman Catholic dialogue helps us relate our offering to that of Christ: 'none is added externally to the offering of Christ, but each derives from Him and points to Him'. We may compare this with Wesley's:

> Jesus this mean oblation join
> to Thy great sacrifice (*HP* 383)

In Holy Communion Methodists plead the completed and eternal sacrifice of Christ, and we offer ourselves anew in and through the eternal sacrifice, but we do not in any

way offer the sacrifice again. At Holy Communion what Methodists do is to make a memorial of and participate in the offering of Christ.

Presence – *"His presence makes the feast"*

172
When Christians talk of the 'real presence' of Christ in Holy Communion they may mean any one or more of a number of things: the general presence of the risen and ascended Christ who is with us always, the presence of Christ as 'invisible host', welcoming us to His table, the presence of Christ in the action of 'breaking bread', the presence of Christ in the act of sharing in the consecrated bread and wine and the fellowship expressed and created by it, and the presence of Christ in the consecrated elements.

173
In the climax of the Easter story of the Road to Emmaus (Luke 24:13-35) the Risen Christ made himself known to his disciples in the breaking of the bread. In the actions of Jesus taking, blessing, breaking and sharing the bread the eyes of his followers were opened and they recognised him. In John 2, at the first sign at Cana in Galilee, it is the gift of new wine in abundance that reveals the glory of God. In Matthew 11:19, in contrast with John the Baptist, Jesus arrives eating and drinking. In 1 Corinthians 11:29 worshippers bring condemnation upon themselves if they fail to discern in the Eucharist the body of Christ. In John 15 there is an intimacy between Christ and his disciples that is described by the total dependence of the branches on the vine.

174
Almost all Christians agree that the risen Christ is present in Holy Communion as 'invisible host', and would recognise him, as did the first disciples in the 'breaking of bread' at Emmaus. Most would also recognise him in the eucharistic community, as they also recognise him 'where two or three are gathered together.' There is continuing disagreement as to whether he can also be said to be present in the consecrated elements of bread and wine (although to most Methodists this is not an issue with which they are greatly concerned and they do not emphasise any particular moment or words in the liturgy as effecting an act of consecration).

175
From very early on, and certainly from the second century, it was generally believed that Christ <u>was</u> present in the consecrated elements. Justin Martyr tells us that the bread and wine after their setting aside are no longer ordinary bread and wine but

are 'Eucharist'. To this day, this view is strongly maintained in the Roman Catholic, Orthodox and Lutheran Churches and also by many Anglicans, though these traditions differ as to the exact language they use to describe the change, the nature of the presence and the point in the liturgy at which this change occurs. At the Reformation, most Protestants, other than Lutherans, denied any essential change in the bread and wine, though they varied as between the Zwinglians who regarded the bread and wine as 'bare signs' and the high Calvinists who maintained that, though the bread and wine remained such, faithful communicants nevertheless truly received the body and blood of Christ in the act of Communion. Today, some who maintain that the bread and wine do not change, nevertheless assert strongly that Christ is dynamically present in the vivid action of breaking and pouring and that it is here rather than in the elements that the 'real presence' is vividly manifested. Clearly, however, it is possible to assert his presence both in the actions and in the elements.

176
The views of the Wesleys appear ambiguous. The hymns talk of the 'tokens', implying a Calvinist doctrine of the presence, but also use such terms as 'mystic bread' and 'everlasting wine'. Charles Wesley's 'no local deity' may indicate a reaction against a strand of Counter-Reformation piety which might have been seen as suggesting that Christ is somehow held 'prisoner' within the consecrated eucharistic bread and wine. Perhaps the Wesleys might have affirmed a recent Lutheran-Roman Catholic formula: 'These terms (i.e. trans- and consubstantiation) have in common a rejection of a spatial or natural manner of presence, and a rejection of an understanding of the sacrament as only commemorative or figurative'. Later Methodists have shared some of this ambiguity. The 1971 Denver report of the international Roman Catholic-Methodist dialogue asserted a joint conviction that 'bread and wine do not mean the same outside of the context of eucharistic celebration as they do in that sacrament' but, at the same time, it recorded a difference over 'the transformation of bread and wine' and that 'Methodists do not consider the transformation to be such that bread and wine cease to be bread and wine'.

177
A concern registered in the British Methodist 'Lima' response related to any belief that the presence of Christ in Holy Communion was somehow 'superior' to His presence in other means of grace. On the one hand, one may say that Methodists are rightly chary of any attempt to 'quantify' grace. On the other hand, it may be said that the institution of varying means of grace corresponds with God's desire to communicate with us in differing ways and according to differing human capacities. In this case, it

can be legitimate to talk of Christ's presence in Holy Communion as 'unique', as indeed Charles Wesley does with 'thine own appointed way.'

178
In dialogue with other world Communions Methodists have stressed their inherited theology on eucharistic sacrifice, on *epiclesis* and on *anamnesis* derived from the hymns of the Wesleys and have suggested that part of the Western and Roman Catholic tradition may have been mistaken in allowing Holy Communion to be 'over-defined'. For instance, the Wesleys affirmed and celebrated the real presence of Christ in Holy Communion but were agnostic about the precise nature of it. In their response to the Lima Report British Methodists shied away from over-commitment to unique modes of Christ's presence. Christ is present according to his promise in the gathered assembly. Christ is also present in the eucharistic action. Each mode of Christ's presence is real and according to his promise but is not ultimately or helpfully definable.

179
Finally, we may note that the United Methodist Church considers that 'the theology of *'anamnesis'* and *'epiclesis'* allows us to transcend any division between the concepts of presence in the bread and wine, presence in the faithful communicants, presence in the dynamic actions of the memorial and corporate presence in the entire body, the Church'. Nevertheless, it is clear that individual Methodists will have widely varying views on the concept of the 'real presence'.

The work of the Spirit *(epiclesis)* – *"Pour out your spirit"*

180
The Holy Spirit is, in the words of Charles Wesley, 'the Divine Remembrancer'. In John 14:26 Jesus says that the Holy Spirit will take what is his and show it to the disciples. Since Holy Communion cannot be separated from the Resurrection of Christ and from Pentecost it must be an event of the Spirit. The body of Christ which is the Church, and the body of Christ which is the Eucharist, cannot be separated. The one Spirit by whom we are all baptised into the one body (1 Corinthians 12:13) is the same Spirit who unites us in and with the body of Christ in Holy Communion. The Holy Spirit at work in the Church of the Acts of the Apostles brings into effect a witnessing and preaching community in which there is apostolic teaching, fellowship, prayer and the breaking of the bread (Acts 2:42). The Holy Spirit, who makes Christ present in the overshadowing of the Virgin Mary, is the same Holy Spirit who makes Christ real to the Church in Holy Communion. *Epiclesis* is not simply the invocation or prayer for the Spirit but in its wider sense is linked with all calling on the name of the Lord.

181

Though the New Testament does not specifically mention the Holy Spirit in connection with Holy Communion, the practice of invoking the Holy Spirit in the context of eucharistic worship can be found in the early rite of Hippolytus (c 215). It is particularly emphasised as the key 'moment' in consecrating the Eucharist in the Eastern tradition. In medieval Western theology, the role of the Spirit was somewhat downplayed, and was not restored by the Reformers. The 1637 Anglican Scottish Liturgy mentions the role of the Spirit in 'sanctifying these gifts'.

182

From the beginning of their dialogues with Roman Catholics and Lutherans Methodists have been glad to affirm a distinctive emphasis on the role of the Holy Spirit in Holy Communion. From the Churches of the East and from the earlier 1549 Prayer Book tradition the Wesleys inherited the notion that the Spirit was to be invoked to make real and true all that God had promised to bestow on the faithful through Holy Communion, as evidenced in the hymns 'Come Holy Ghost, thine influence shed' (*HP* 602) and 'Come, thou everlasting Spirit' (*HP* 298). For the Wesleys the Spirit of God was not in opposition to matter and to material things. Therefore the authentic Methodist position in ecumenical dialogue is that the Spirit employs the eucharistic bread and wine to convey the gift of divine love to every faithful heart. The Methodist witness is that the promised Spirit, the true disciple rightly believing and the elements rightly set forth are all essential requirements of Holy Communion.

183

The Liturgical Movement led to a renewed emphasis on the role of the Spirit as making Christ crucified and risen present to the worshipping congregation in Holy Communion. The Canadian Anglican response to the 'Lima' document specified that an *epiclesis* 'makes it clear that the sacraments are prayer actions and not mechanical means of grace'. An *epiclesis* was incorporated into the Lord's Supper in the *Methodist Service Book* and even more strongly into the services of the *Methodist Worship Book*. The Lima text saw invocation of the Spirit as one of the five main themes of Holy Communion, arguing that though 'the presence of Christ is clearly the centre of the Eucharist', it is 'the Father who is the primary origin and final fulfilment of the eucharistic event' and the Holy Spirit 'is the immeasurable strength of love which makes it possible and continues to make it effective'.

184

Within the theology of Holy Communion, there are varying degrees of emphasis on

the role of the Spirit in effecting the 'consecration' of the elements and the binding together of the communicants as the 'body of Christ'. The *epiclesis* for the first service of Holy Communion in Ordinary Seasons in the *Methodist Worship Book* reads:

> Send down your Holy Spirit
> that these gifts of bread and wine
> may be for us the body and blood of Christ.
> Unite us with him for ever
> and bring us with the whole creation
> to your eternal kingdom

Reactions to the draft services that preceded the *Methodist Worship Book* revealed a division of opinion between those who felt it was legitimate to invoke the Spirit on the 'inanimate objects' of bread and wine and those who did not accept this. The compilers and the Conference were at pains to produce a fairly standard form for the *epiclesis* that contained the classical Wesleyan ambiguity in a prayer for the Spirit to descend on both the gifts and the people. However, Methodists do not emphasise any *particular* moment or words in the liturgy as effecting an 'act of consecration'. Though there is very widespread emphasis ecumenically upon the role of the Spirit as 'remembrancer divine' in Holy Communion, some find difficulty with the concept of the Spirit's action upon the elements rather than upon the hearts of believers. One may suggest that the Spirit does act upon the whole of creation (c.f. Genesis 1 and Psalm 104). The role of the Spirit is also linked to the eschatological understanding of Holy Communion, discussed below.

Anticipation (Eschatology) – *"A foretaste of the heavenly banquet"*

185

At the Last Supper with his disciples Jesus looked forward to drinking the wine anew in the coming kingdom (Luke 22:15-16). The Eucharist in the New Testament is already past, present and future because it looks back to the Exodus, it interprets the Cross as the moment of Christ's sacrifice, and it is an event that the Church is to repeat in the future in order to participate in the benefits of the death of Christ. The Eucharist in the New Testament was a participation in the action of God in Christ in the final age, in the last time, in the days when all history was about to be fulfilled and consummated. In Luke's account of the Last Supper Jesus also promises that those who endure with him will sit at the table of the coming kingdom (Luke 22:30). This motif is also present in the parables about the feasting in the kingdom (Luke 14:16-24; Matthew 22:11-14; Matthew 25:1-13). A similar theme is already present in Isaiah 25:6ff and in the Jewish apocalyptic

conception of fellowship with God being a heavenly banquet (1 Enoch 62:14 and Baruch 29:4-8). Paul taught the first Christians to continue celebrating Holy Communion in an unbroken tradition until the Church met Christ in glory (1 Corinthians 11:26). The cry of the early Church *Marana tha* is a prayer for Christ to be present in worship now and to come to meet the Church in glory. In the Book of Revelation the final picture of the kingdom is the marriage feast of the Lamb: Christ and his Church, bridegroom and bride will exchange their fasting for feasting. In the Book of Revelation Christ brings the faithful to final rest and nourishment.

186
From the earliest days of the Church, Holy Communion appears to have been celebrated with an eye on the *eschaton*. The *Didache* contains prayers vibrant with eschatological expectation. Thus we read:

> Remember, Lord, your Church ... bring it together from the four winds, now sanctified, into your kingdom, which you have prepared for it ... May grace come and let this world pass away.

Holy Communion was seen, in varying degrees, in the writings of the early fathers and in many of the early liturgies as foreshadowing the eschatological banquet of the Kingdom to come. St Maximus the Confessor (580-662) referred to the Eucharist as the 'memorial of the things to come'. The eschatological understanding and orientation remained strong in the Eastern Christian tradition while becoming less prominent in the West.

187
The Wesleys gave importance to the relationship between Eucharist and eschatology. The feast of Christ truly present with his people is a foretaste of the feast of the final ingathering of God's holy people drawn from every nation into a kingdom of justice and righteousness. They devoted a whole section of their '*Hymns on the Lord's Supper*' to 'the sacrament as a pledge of heaven'. They talk of the Supper as the 'type of the heavenly marriage feast' and use the terms, 'pledge', 'earnest' and 'taste of the fullness'. We may quote just a few lines from hymn 93:

> The wine that doth His passion show,
> We soon with Him shall drink it new
> in yonder dazzling courts above.

and

> by faith and hope already there
> even now the marriage feast we share.

The Wesleys emphasise however that this is not yet the fullness:

Nourished on earth with living bread.

188
Studies of the responses to the 'Lima' text of 1982 reveal widespread approval of the current emphasis on Holy Communion as 'foretaste of the heavenly banquet'. This central eucharistic theme, often dormant in the history of the Church, has been revived in recent years, not least by the Lima statement and those who have written on Holy Communion and human liberation.

Mission and justice – *"To live and work to God's praise and glory"*

189
The 'daily bread' for which Christ taught his disciples to pray can be understood as a prayer for justice for all and provision for all both here and hereafter. The feeding of the five thousand in John 6 begins as the Messiah feeding God's hungry children in the wilderness, but develops into a discourse on the true and living bread and finally Jesus is inviting the faithful to feed on him in Holy Communion. Here is the theme newly studied in our own time under the heading 'Eucharist and liberation'. The sacrifice of which God approves is a sharing with those in need (Hebrews 13:16, Acts 2:44 and Acts 4:32). In the Johannine epistles, the Church cannot have communion with the Father, through the Son, if it is not in communion with others and itself. This accords with the prophetic tradition of Isaiah and Micah, which condemns all who seek to worship with ritual sacrifice while they trample on the poor and marginalized. (Similarly, in Genesis 31:54f the reconciliation between Laban and Jacob is sealed in the sharing of a meal.) Eucharist in the New Testament is about right relationships (1 Corinthians 11:28). Gifts cannot be brought to the altar by those who are not reconciled. The eucharistic community of Acts 2:44f is a sharing community in which the basic needs of all are met. As an expression of this, the eucharistic assembly collects money for the poor (2 Corinthians 9:13, 2 Corinthians 8:3-4 and Romans 15:26-37).

190
We can see, then, that from the earliest times Holy Communion has been seen as implying a personal and corporate commitment to mission and justice. Christians cannot but wish to shout from the rooftops the Gospel that they proclaim in word and Eucharist. In order to render their fellowship a credible sign before the world, they have to live in accordance with the implications of Holy Communion. Paul saw a failure to

realise the social justice implications of eucharistic living within their own fellowship as a 'failure to discern the body', both the sacramental body of the Lord and his servant Body of the Church being linked in this judgement. Later, St John Chrysostom referred to the duty of Christians to go out and 'celebrate the Liturgy after the Liturgy' by which he meant the service of Christ in the poor and needy after the celebration of Christ in the sacrament. Liturgical revisions in recent years have emphasised the commitment to live out the faith in the world. To cite but one, the *Methodist Worship Book's* first service for Holy Communion in Ordinary Seasons ends with the command:

> Go in peace in the power of the Spirit
> to live and work to God's praise and glory

191
The Eastern Christian tradition has particularly emphasised the consequences for Christian lifestyle of Holy Communion. A eucharistic lifestyle, in which the emphasis is on praise and sharing is in opposition to a consumerist one – it is a life-style that has radical implications for peace, justice and the integrity of creation in terms of conservation and ecology. These insights are now generally accepted within practically all sections of the contemporary Church.

Personal devotion – *"Bread to pilgrims given"*

192
In almost all Christian traditions, receiving Holy Communion is seen as a very significant element in Christian devotion, whether it is received very frequently, as by many Roman Catholics and Anglicans, or relatively rarely, as in some Scottish Reformed traditions. Christ, like Moses and Elijah before him, must feed the people as the agent of God's great work. The theology of John 6 moves from the feeding in the desert to feeding on Christ himself. Christ is the living bread who has come down from heaven. The Church is to find its nourishment by feeding on him. The charge to Peter is to feed the flock (John 21).

193
The late medieval Western Roman Catholic tradition developed elaborate forms of eucharistic devotion that were generally repudiated in the Reformation traditions. Formerly, eucharistic Communion was reserved in almost all traditions to those initiated into full membership. In the early Church, catechumens were dismissed after the service of the word and not allowed to witness the Great Prayer of Thanksgiving, let alone receive Communion.

194

When John Wesley saw Holy Communion as a 'converting ordinance', he did so in the context of a serious search for salvation. He assumed that the 'unconverted' who came to Holy Communion would be members of the societies, 'desiring to flee from the wrath to come' and would have assumed a very serious search for God. He believed that, within the context of experiencing the vividness of the sign, the 'penny would drop' for many and they would receive the necessary assurance that Christ had indeed died for them and achieved their salvation. Most Methodists would still feel that Wesley's approach was valid and that whatever the Church's discipline over eucharistic Communion, it should never exclude those who come with the serious intention that Wesley assumed. Many might feel that, to the extent that Holy Communion commemorates Christ's openness to sinners, such an approach is eminently defensible.

Discussion questions: Looking back at the nine themes considered in this section of the report, how important is each of them to you? And why?

Does this section offer you any helpful new ways of thinking about Holy Communion? Is there a difference between your personal views and those of others in your church (bearing in mind what is said in paragraphs 157-162 about 'koinonia')?

How does our understanding of the meaning of Holy Communion affect the way we might celebrate it?

(iii) The origins of Holy Communion

195

Only in the twentieth century did the Christian Churches, including Methodism, become exposed to a rigorous investigative scholarship that put an end to persistent romanticism about the origins and early development of eucharistic faith and practice. Everyone now concedes the limitations imposed upon us by having no written evidence outside the New Testament about the details of first century Jewish synagogue worship or Jewish fellowship meals. There are few, if any, surviving Jewish liturgical texts from before the 8th century, and the form of celebration of Holy Communion in the New Testament is not recoverable.

196
For a long time the early Christian Eucharist was a private gathering of no more than could be got into one house – large or small, as the case may be – probably about seventy worshippers at the most. The identity of those present may often have been a closely guarded secret, for fear of persecution. The uniqueness of the communion-fellowship meal was the participation in it of all initiated believers regardless of gender, ethnic origin or social status. Ritual corporate communion-fellowship meals were common to Jews, Christians and pagans alike.

197
The original relationship of the Christian Eucharist to the Passover is not clear. Holy Communion as it relates to the death of Christ has strong Passover theology within it, but in many ways it has more parallels with regular Jewish liturgical Seder meals and with the weekly Sabbath celebratory meal than with the Passover. However, these Jewish meals are celebrated in private homes rather than in a public place of worship, which ultimately became the norm for the Christian Eucharist. The mention of two cups in some versions of Luke's gospel may imply that what were later distinct types of Christian meal, the Lord's Supper and the *agape*, in some congregations were at that time still an intrinsic whole. On the other hand, a Christian ritual proclaiming the Lord's death and a fellowship meal celebrating the presence of the risen Christ in the midst of the disciples may reflect different emphases in one part of the Church from another. The evidence is, however, inconclusive.

198
Other Jewish antecedents with heavy links to the Lord's Supper include the threefold Jewish *Birkat ha-Mazon*, of blessing, thanksgiving and petition, recited over the final Seder cup and the eschatological prayer for the coming of the Messiah.

199
We have no substantial surviving written accounts of synagogue worship in New Testament times or in the early patristic period. However it seems probable that psalmody, scripture and prayers were strong features and that they form a parallel with the origins of the 'Service of the Word', the first part of the developing Christian Eucharist described in outline by Justin Martyr in the middle of the 2nd century.

200
The oldest surviving eucharistic prayer or Great Thanksgiving dates from around the year 215 and comes from the hand of the Roman presbyter, Hippolytus. Hippolytus is

providing an aide-memoire for bishops whose extempore prayer was either too lengthy or lacking in theological competence. Due to lack of other contemporary accounts of the content of the Great Prayer the Hippolytan form of the prayer has had enormous influence on the composition of eucharistic prayers in recent years.

201
Traditionally, in both the east and the west, but in varying order, the eucharistic prayer had a common structure and came to consist of most of the following elements: the opening dialogue, thanksgiving for creation and redemption, the Sanctus ('Holy, Holy, Holy ...'), the account of the institution of the Lord's Supper, the proclamation of the memorial act, a prayer invoking the Holy Spirit on the people and the gifts, a brief act of intercession, a final doxology and a concluding 'Amen'.

202
In most versions of the eucharistic prayer, there was a recital of the institution narrative. The various versions of the narrative were either parallels with, or amalgams of, the four New Testament accounts – namely words and phrases drawn from Matthew 26:17-30, Mark 14:12-26, Luke 22:7-23 and 1 Corinthians 11:23-26. As to which of the words, apart from 'This [is] my body' and 'This [is] my blood' go back to Jesus himself, scholars cannot agree. The New Testament institution narratives concentrate on the death of Christ rather than the resurrection.

(iv) Eucharistic theology in recent years

203
In recent years, much eucharistic theology has discussed the notion of Holy Communion forming a sacramental community. In the 1960s, the Second Vatican Council spoke of Christ being the sacrament of God's presence and of the Church being a sacrament in itself derived from Christ 'the primal sacrament'. Fifty years before this the Methodist theologian Ryder Smith had spoken of the Church as 'the sacramental society'. The Church as the Body of Christ is brought into being and formed by both word and sacrament. Although it is an over-simplification to do so, we might say that those world Communions that have given a lesser significance to Holy Communion itself have tended to speak of the Church being constituted and formed by the Word of God, read and preached, whilst by contrast, those that have given a lesser place to the ministry of the word have claimed that the Body of Christ is formed pre-eminently by the Eucharist. Methodists would want to align themselves with the current ecumenical insistence that the Body of Christ is formed,

perhaps equally, by the nourishment it receives from both Word and Table. Certainly it is above all in worship that Christ himself is formed in us – severally and together. It is in worship that in Wesley's words we grow together 'in full conformity to our exalted Head'

204
Another contemporary ecumenical theme, now embraced by many Methodists but not an issue in the time of the Wesleys, is what is often referred to as 'embodied' worship. In language familiar to Methodists this would be called 'the mystic harmony linking sense to sound and sight' (*HP* 333). Those who are participants in Holy Communion are not disembodied spirits indifferent to sight and sound – unaffected by the incarnation or by the classic drama of colour and movement of the liturgy. The liturgical movement – an integrated parallel with the ecumenical movement – has encouraged Christians to think about the layout of their churches. The arrangement of the worship space is a key part of Holy Communion – of word and sacrament. The cycle of the Christian year is an annual recapitulation of the saving acts of God in Christ proclaimed in story, music, colour, movement, light, and symbol.

Postscript

205
As we have already noted, Holy Communion is an aspect of the Church's life which has grown in significance for Methodists in the past thirty years. Indeed, the 2001 National Church Life Survey, which questioned a sample of around 10% of all those worshipping in Methodist churches in England on the day of the national census, revealed, perhaps surprisingly, that Holy Communion was valued more highly than preaching. It is to be hoped that, by receiving the insights of others, and drawing upon the riches of our own and other traditions, we may continue to grow in appreciation of our Lord's gracious gift in this Sacrament.

Because thou hast said:
'Do this for my sake',
The mystical bread
We gladly partake;
We thirst for the Spirit
That flows from above,
And long to inherit
Thy fullness of love.

'Tis here we look up
And grasp at thy mind;
'Tis here that we hope
Thine image to find;
The means of bestowing
Thy gifts we embrace;
But all things are owing
To Jesus's grace.

Charles Wesley (1707-1788) alt
Hymns & Psalms 598

Discussion questions: In what ways has your thinking about Holy Communion been confirmed, challenged or changed by reading this report? How might this affect your practice?

What would you now like to talk about more with others?

H GLOSSARY

***Agape* ('Love Feast')** A common meal shared by Christians in which the presence of the risen Lord was joyfully celebrated.

Anamnesis See paragraphs 157-161.

Arminianism A theological emphasis propounded by Joseph Arminius (1560-1609), which stresses the availability of God's grace for all humanity. It explicitly rejects all forms of 'pre-destination' (the belief that some are pre-destined by God to be saved, others to be lost), and became a strong component of the theology of John Wesley.

Cassock-alb A white ankle-length tunic with long narrow sleeves and a girdle or belt at the waist, possibly hooded, worn by a minister presiding at the eucharist. It is derived from the clothing worn by professional people in classical times.

Chalice A large cup used for the wine in a service of Holy Communion, usually made of silver. In Methodist churches, the chalice may be empty, or used by the presiding minister alone, rather than passed around all those taking part.

Communion

(1) 'Holy Communion' The service of Word and Sacrament in which bread and wine are shared, derived from the Last Supper of Jesus before his crucifixion.

(2) One of the worldwide families/denominations of churches sharing common origins and doctrinal emphases, e.g. Methodist, Roman Catholic, Lutheran.

(3) (as in 'inter-' or 'full' 'communion') Sharing in eucharistic hospitality between churches of different denominations.

Consecration The setting apart of bread and wine to be the body and blood of Christ by invocation of the Holy Spirit.

Creed A formalised statement of Christian belief, usually used of those texts agreed by the early Church, such as the Nicene-Constantinopolitan Creed (usually known as the Nicene Creed) of 381.

Didache A Christian text dating from the late first or second century, which describes some of the liturgical practice of the time.

Doxology An expression of praise (literally 'words of glory'), usually Trinitarian in form.

Ecclesiology The study of the nature of the Church (Greek '*ekklesia*').

Elements The bread and wine used in Holy Communion.

Epiclesis (literally 'invocation') The prayer for the consecration of the bread and wine and of the congregation within the Great Prayer of Thanksgiving.

Eschaton (literally 'the last thing') The end of time or of human history.

Eschatology Beliefs about what is to happen at the end of human history (eschaton) and its significance in the present.

Eucharist (literally 'thanksgiving') One of the titles for Holy Communion.

Eucharistic Prayer The great prayer offered by the presiding minister at the eucharist, incorporating elements of thanksgiving, anamnesis, invocation, consecration and doxology.

Eucharistic Sacrifice See paragraph 166.

Fraction The ceremonial breaking of the eucharistic bread for distribution.

Great (Prayer of) Thanksgiving An alternative name for the Eucharistic Prayer.

Institution Narrative A part of the service of Holy Communion, telling the story of its origins in the events of the Last Supper.

Koinonia The Greek word for 'fellowship'/'communion'.

Last Supper The meal shared by Jesus with his disciples on the evening before his crucifixion.

Lima Report The 1982 World Council of Churches Report *Baptism, Eucharist and Ministry*, which attempted to outline areas of theological and liturgical convergence amongst the member churches.

Liturgy (literally, 'work of the people') Worship and prayer, particularly when this is contained in formalised texts.

Lord's Supper One of the titles for Holy Communion, which particularly emphasises the recorded words of Jesus at the Last Supper to 'do this in memory of me'.

Marana tha An Aramaic phrase meaning 'O Lord, come', used in the early church to express a deep longing for Christ's return.

Mass One of the titles for Holy Communion, particularly used in the Roman Catholic Church. The name derives from the Latin verb *mittere* 'to send (away)', used in the words of dismissal *('Ite, missa est.')* traditionally said by the priest at the end of the service.

Maundy Thursday The Thursday in Holy Week, preceding Good Friday, which in particular commemorates the Last Supper.

Oblation A synonym for 'offering'.

Offertory The moment in a service of Holy Communion when bread and wine (and usually the monetary gifts of the people) are formally presented to the presiding minister, or prepared for use.

Ordinary Seasons The periods in the Christian yearly cycle outside the major seasons of Advent, Christmas and Epiphany, Lent, Passiontide, Easter and Pentecost.

Peace A formalised greeting exchanged by presiding minister and some or all of those present at a service of Holy Communion, by words, handshake or token kiss.

Prayer of Humble Access A prayer expressing the unworthiness of participants in Holy Communion to come before the Lord, save through God's grace and mercy.

Presbyter A member of one of the orders of ministry (of which there are currently two in the Methodist Church) who is ordained to the ministry of Word and Sacrament. The term is derived from the Greek word meaning 'elder'. Known as 'priests' in some traditions.

President The minister who leads the service of Holy Communion.

Rubric A ceremonial directions for the conduct of a service, printed alongside the actual text of the prayers, etc.

Sacerdotalist The belief that ordained priests are endowed with sacramental or sacrificial powers. This is explicitly rejected by the Methodist Church's doctrinal standards.

Sacrament See paragraph 140.

Sacramentalist A person whose devotional life places accords great value and emphasis to the sacraments and their associated rituals.

Sacrifice An act of costly giving.

Seder (literally 'order') A ceremonial meal in the Jewish tradition, particularly for observing Sabbath and Passover rituals.

Stole A plain or embroidered scarf-like strip of material worn over the shoulders and over the cassock/alb by ministers, particularly when presiding at a service of Holy Communion. Stoles may be of different colours according to the season of the Christian year.

Synoptic (literally 'with the same eyes') A term used of the Gospels of Matthew, Mark and Luke, which share much material in common.

Vatican II The Second Vatican Council of the Roman Catholic Church, 1962-1965, summoned by Pope John XXIII to consider the spiritual renewal of the Church and its purpose in the modern world. It made many far-reaching decisions affecting the life of the whole Roman Catholic Church.

Vestments Distinctive clothes worn by those leading worship, such as cassock, stole, alb.

I SUGGESTED FURTHER READING

*(Books marked thus * are an easy introduction)*

Ole E. Borgen	*John Wesley on the Sacraments* (Nashville: Abingdon Press 1972)
John C. Bowmer	*The Sacrament of the Lord's Supper in Early Methodism* (London: Dacre Press 1951)
John C. Bowmer	*The Lord's Supper in Methodism*, 1791-1960 (London: Epworth Press 1960)
Paul Bradshaw*	*Early Christian Worship* (London: SPCK 1996) Paul Bradshaw *The Search for the Origins of Christian Worship* (2nd edn.; London: SPCK 2002)
Christopher J. Cocksworth	*Evangelical Eucharistic Thought in the Church of England* (Cambridge: Cambridge University Press 1993)
Neil Dixon*	*Wonder, Love and Praise: a companion to the Methodist Worship Book* (Peterborough: Epworth Press 2003)
Franz Hildebrandt	*I Offered Christ: A Protestant Study of the Mass* (London: Epworth Press 1967)
Joachim Jeremias	*The Eucharistic Words of Jesus* (E.T. of 3rd edn.; London: SCM Press 1966)
I. Howard Marshall	*Last Supper and Lord's Supper* (Exeter: Paternoster Press 1980)
Methodist Worship Book	(Peterborough: Methodist Publishing House 1999)
Max Thurian and Geoffrey Wainwright eds.	*Baptism and Eucharist*: Ecumenical Convergence (Geneva: World Council of Churches 1983)
Michael J. Townsend*	*The Sacraments* (Peterborough: Epworth Press 1999)
Geoffrey Wainwright	*Eucharist and Eschatology* (London: Epworth Press 1971; re-issued Peterborough: Epworth Press 2003)
Geoffrey Wainwright	*Worship with One Accord* (Oxford, New York and Don Mills, ON: Oxford University Press 1997)

Geoffrey Wainwright	*Worship with One Accord* (Oxford, New York and Don Mills, ON: Oxford University Press 1997)
Gordon S. Wakefield	*An Outline of Christian Worship* (Edinburgh: T & T Clark 1998)
Gordon S. Wakefield*	*Methodist Spirituality* (Peterborough: Epworth Press 2000)
John and Charles Wesley	*Hymns on the Lord's Supper* Bristol 1745 Facsimile Reprint: Chas. Wesley Society, Madison NJ 1995
James F. White*	*Introduction to Christian Worship* (3rd edn.; Nashville: Abingdon Press 2002)
James F. White	*The Sacraments in Protestant Practice and Faith* (Nashville: Abingdon Press 1999)
Susan J. White*	*Groundwork of Christian Worship* (Peterborough: Epworth Press 1997)
World Council of Churches*	*Baptism, Eucharist and Ministry* (The Lima Report; Geneva: World Council of Churches 1982)

J RESOLUTIONS

10/4. The Conference receives the Report.

10/5. The Conference commends the Report to Districts, Circuits and local churches for study and comments and invites responses to be sent to the Faith and Order Secretary by 31st October 2004, and directs the Faith and Order Committee to report on the responses received to the Conference of 2005.

10/6. The Conference encourages ministers, those with responsibility for ministerial formation and continuing development and all other Methodists to reflect upon their beliefs and practices regarding the celebration of the Lord's Supper in the light of this Report and the Guidance for Ordering a Service of Holy Communion in the *Methodist Worship Book*.